Someday I'm Going to . . .

Brad Rudisail

DEDICATION

This book is dedicated to all of the dreamers of the world that help make the world the wonderment it is today.

CONTENTS

Seventeen months ago I was sitting in a counselor's office, searching for some rapid insight into how to take back control of my life. I had two mortgages, three jobs, a two plus hour commute every day and a nervous breakdown that seemed imminent.

As I left her office and walked across the parking lot towards my vehicle, I asked myself, "How did I let it get this crazy? I can't keep this up forever."

Then I said those words,

"Someday I'm going to . . . ."

. . . . And a book was born

   -   Brad Rudisail

ACKNOWLEDGMENTS

Thanks to Amjad Shahzad for the wonderful cover that captures the essence of the book

Thanks to Jill Hartman-Roberts who did a spectacular job editing many of the chapters of this book

Thanks to the other members of the AWA who helped edit and shape the book including Zhanna, Jennifer, Sharon and Nancy.

Thanks to Gus and Linda for their story contributions

Thanks to you for spending your hard earned money on this book.

When is Someday Ever Going to Come?

"Someday. That's a dangerous word. It's really just a code for never"

-   Tom Cruise as Roy Miller in "*Knight and Day*"

When is Someday ever going to come?

No, not Sunday, Someday.

You know that day. You've dreamt and talked about it all these years. You think about that day as you're driving to work. You think about that day when you fall into bed after a hard day on the job, or after another infuriating foray with your spouse. You talk about it over a glass of wine or a couple of drinks at the bar on a Friday night. It's an aspiration, it's a dream, and it's an escape. It's a day that has great importance to you.

It's the opening statement of a mantra, a mantra that you have said to yourself over and over again all these years. I'm not sure of the exact wording of this mantra, but I imagine it is something like:

"Someday, I'm going to go to Europe and see the Eiffel Tower, or walk the streets of Italy or share a pint with the locals in Ireland."

3

"Someday, I'm going to write a book or learn a musical instrument."

"Someday, I'm going to quit this job that brings me little satisfaction and pursue something on my own that I'm passionate about."

"Someday I'm going to get out of debt."

"Someday I'm going to get out of this dead end relationship and find someone who is crazy about me and will love me emphatically."

"Someday I'm going to have the body I've always wanted."

"Someday I'm going to _____."

Sound familiar?

Someday you're going to "blank."

Your friends and family know all about your Someday. They've tirelessly heard you talk about it all these years over and over again.

They've heard you talk about your dreams of starting your own business one day every Friday at those after work get-togethers when you all have a few drinks to kick off the weekend. Every week they've heard you complain about the job where both you and your efforts are underappreciated and every week they hear you proclaim yet again how you are going to walk into your obnoxious boss's office and quit your job Someday.

They've heard you complain about your spouse time and time again. They always sympathize with you about how your spouse shows you no respect anymore and displays little or no romantic interest in you now. They've heard you reiterate the continual stories of how he or she came home drunk last night again, or how they continue to verbally cut down your ideas and dreams. They hear you yet again proclaim that you are going to leave your spouse Someday and find someone who truly loves, adores and respects you.

They've heard your ideas for a book you want to write, the invention you have conceived in your mind or the secret opportunity you know about that is going to make you a mint "Someday."

Yes, they've heard all about Someday. They've heard you audibly declare your mantra more times than they'd care to. The fact is that your friends are waiting for Someday to come as well, so that you'll move on with your life and they can stop hearing about it. They are weary of you affirming your Someday verbally. They are ready to see your actions affirm it.

What are you waiting on?

Do you want to be talking about Someday a year from now? Five years from now? Ten?

Or do you want to be walking the streets of Europe?

Do you want to be working for yourself doing something you truly love?

Be wrapped up in the arms of someone who is completely in love with you?

Be putting the last finishing touches on that book?

Or feeling the power of that bike beneath you as you experience the invigoration of the wind in your face as you navigate those mountain roads on your bike.

Here is the cold hard truth. Until you actually DO SOMETHING, Someday is never going to come.

At some point, and maybe that point is now, no one is going to take your Someday seriously anymore, not even yourself.

Nothing is going to magically make things happen for you.

Only you can do it!

That is what this book is about. It's about Someday, and how to make it happen for you, instead of merely talking about it. Talking about something is easy, which is why so many people just talk about it.

Doing something about it requires commitment and dedication to see it through. It sometimes requires tough decisions to be made and uncomfortable steps to be taken. It requires that you constantly move forward to seeing it through. In the blockbuster zombie movie, World War Z, Brad Pitt's character makes a profound statement that defines the theme of the movie, "Movement is life."

Movement is indeed life. Talking about it is what old men do at the senior center as they regretfully admit the opportunities they failed to act on earlier in life.

Stop talking, start doing, and get on with your life!

You've got a Someday to live soon.

Two Deadly Words

"You take the blue pill, the story ends, you wake up in your bed and believe whatever you want to believe. You take the red pill, you stay in Wonderland, and I show you how deep the rabbit hole goes."

- Lawrence Fishburne as Morpheus in *The Matrix*

You may remember from your high school chemistry course that the ordinary table salt you use every day to improve the taste of your food is made up of two deadly poisons; sodium and chlorine. Imagine that, two lethal elements come together to form a compound that not only doesn't kill us, it actually adds aesthetic value to our lives. It makes our food taste better, and since food is such a primary part of our lives, these two toxic elements actually improve our lives when used in conjunction with one another.

In the English language there are two words that when used singularly or isolated from one another, are useful wonderful words. But when they are used in conjunction with one another they form a deadly phrasing compound.

I'm sure you've uttered these two words in succession. They seem innocent enough. It seems perfectly logical to use these two words as a pair. And once I point out the dangerous oxymoron that these two words make up, you will realize that you've probably used them more times than you will care to admit.

These two words are an evasion that help ensure that Someday never comes.

Are you ready for these two words?

Here they are:

"I should."

And after today, you need to wipe these two words from your vocabulary!

So what is so terrible about this phrase? It's because like an iceberg, you don't see the entire object. It's not the visible part of the iceberg that sinks ships. It's the part that lies hidden underneath the ocean that rips a tear in the hull, sending the ship to its watery grave, and sometimes the crew as well.

"I should," has an invisible element as well. "I should" is actually the visible part of a five word phrase and it's the hidden aspect of it that is holding you back from seeing your Someday through.

You see, "I should" is invisibly followed by "but I won't"

When you utter the words "I should," you are really saying "I should, but I won't."

When you use that phrase with someone in a

conversation, what you are saying is, "I agree with you, but I'm not going to do that."

Maybe a friend of yours at one time suggested that you scale down your life and decrease the size of your overhead because the financial pressure of having to meet all those payments prevents you from enjoying life and you said, "I should (but I won't)."

And now five years has passed and the bills are still mounting to support your overly large home, your two new cars and the store size selection of clothes in your master bedroom closet. You find yourself working all the time, which keeps you away from your family or simply relaxing on a lazy weekend.

Maybe you've reiterated the news to your family that your doctor gave you that you need to start losing weight before it starts impacting your health down the road, and when your family asks you if you will indeed follow the doctor's advice, you answered, "I should (but I won't)."

And now ten years later, you are even more overweight and your back aches every morning and your feet hurt at the end of every day as they are forced to support your ever increasing weight.

Maybe you have a confidant in your inner circle that you share the intimate details about your marriage and how awful it is. You tell them how they continue to verbally abuse you, especially after they've been drinking. You reiterate how they show you disrespect and display no appreciation for you. Your confidant suggests that you talk to an attorney and look into the possibility of leaving this horrible person to which you tell them, "Yes, I should, (but I won't)

And ten years later you are still with this miserable person, in a miserable marriage, and your life is even more miserable than it was ten years ago, while you continue to complain.

Do you see the pattern?

Listen for those two words when you converse with other people. You will hear them now with an entirely new viewpoint. You will discern the negative connation those two words convey when friends and acquaintances use them together in conversation. You will no longer optimistically interpret that phrase from others as a commitment of action and garner false hope when you hear those words uttered by those you care about. That is because you will be able to see the three words that reside below the surface, the three words that complete the empty submissive nature of that phrase.

As for yourself, you need to omit those two words from your vocabulary starting right now.

It's time to change "I should" to "I will."

Say the phrase, "I will do that." Do you feel how much more positive those words sound together? Do you feel how much energy is behind that statement? "I will" is an affirmation. It is a statement confirming that you are going to indeed implement the advice that was thoughtfully laid out for you.   With that simple confirmation, you are pointing your sword towards the horizon, as you prepare to charge ahead towards your goal, towards your Someday.

One doesn't usually accomplish an end goal in one dramatic step.   The journey to your Someday will encompass a lot of baby steps along the way, after all, you have years of procrastination and apathy to overcome. Inertia has set in and planted roots around you, making it difficult to move and create momentum. But making little changes in your life, such as converting an "I should" to an "I will" will give you the energy to get past that inertia and build up momentum until pretty soon, you are steamrolling towards your goal.

Can you do that?

Yes, I will!

Someday I Will Talk to a Stranger

"Courage is not the absence of fear, but rather the judgment that something else is more important than fear."

- Ambrose Redmoon, Author, *No Peaceful Warriors!*

I will never forget those days in elementary school when the teacher would go row by row, asking each student to read a paragraph from the text book. As soon as the teacher called on the first student and I discerned what her likely row pattern would be, I would count the number of students in front of me, and then count the number of paragraphs to see which one I would be delegated to read. As I did so, I would pray that it would be a short paragraph and be void of any words that started with an "f" or a "p". Those were the worst. Once I found my paragraph, I would read each word over and over again in my mind, picturing myself reading them fluently and clearly. As my turn drew nearer, my heart would beat faster. By the time it was my turn to read, I was a nervous wreck.

This is the typical saga in the daily life of a child afflicted with a stuttering problem. I have read many stories of children fainting as their turn to read drew near in this same circumstance. The worst classroom dramas were originated from teachers who would simply arbitrarily call on students to read the next paragraph. I would spend the entire time sinking as low as I could in my desk, hoping that the teacher wouldn't notice me.

The fear of stuttering in front of your peers is daunting and unnerving. Every time you open your mouth, you expose yourself and make yourself susceptible to mockery, embarrassment and ridicule. On a website where young people can anonymously post their thoughts and experiences with their stuttering, one young man wrote:

> *"I don't want to go to school because I stutter and I can't say my name, I don't want to have to say it in front of teachers! Everyone will laugh at me like they did in Math and English. In Math the teacher asked for my name and everybody laughed. In English, I had to perform a skit in-front of the class and everybody laughed!! I don't want to go back to school!"*

My father pushed me to become involved in a number of things despite my impediment, one of them being Boy Scouts. I loved the scouts and as typical of my Capricorn qualities, I immediately set my goal of becoming an Eagle Scout one day. The first step of the long journey was to make Tenderfoot, for which you needed two skill awards and a merit badge. I studied and obtained my two skill awards within a couple of months, but I never got that merit badge. I never did because in order to get the merit badge, you had to call Mr. Fuller on the phone, and his name started with an "F." I never did call Mr. Fuller, and I never got that merit badge, and 14 months later, I dropped out of scouts.

The telephone is terrifying for a stutterer. During a physical conversation, the other person can at least see you and empathize with your struggle to converse. They can read your body language and see you as a real person. On the phone however, you only have your voice to represent you, which is your weakest asset. How I wish I had access to texting or email when I was growing up. It would have been so much easier.

I remember in high school when I would decide to make the effort to ask a girl out for a date. I would begin the drama of making that call at about seven o'clock in the evening. Much of the first hour was spent staring at the phone, pacing back and forth in my room and rehearsing what I would say. I would practice my prearranged lines for every circumstance that would occur, should Carrie herself answer the phone or her mom, dad, or a sibling. This was in the days before cell phones so you never knew who would answer the phone. By 8:15 I would pick the phone up for the first time, only to put it back in its cradle. Sometimes I would press the first few digits of her phone number, and then terminate the process. This charade would continue until I would finally make the call at 9:45 only to have Carrie tell me that she couldn't go out.

Somewhere within every detriment is a silver lining however, and because of my speech impediment, I became very good at two things, writing and playing the piano. I would spend hours down in the basement, playing my Rhodes electric piano, letting the piano keys verbalize my thoughts. My piano and I would talk about the rough day I had endured at school, my dreams of the future, and my desire to go out with that cute girl in my third period class. And as I would get lost in my music, I would say to myself:

"Someday, I'm going to perform for an audience, and not be afraid to talk to them between songs."

"Someday, I'm going to speak without worry, without fear, without anxiety or trepidation."

"Someday, I will welcome the opportunity to speak."

The beautiful thing is that all of those Somedays came true, and one of the reasons was my enrollment in the Hollins Speech Institute in my mid 20's. The Hollins Institute is a world famous clinic which has had much success in helping people overcome their stuttering affliction. It is a 21-day intensive program that basically retrains one how to talk. By the start of the third week, patients are speaking far more fluently. The transformation process is startling. It is at that time that the therapists start to push the students and force them out into every day speaking situations.

All stutterers accept some degree of avoidance and compromise in their lives. Many have never stopped to ask for directions, they've never asked the store clerk if that sweater comes in a large. They choose a career field such as accounting or computer programming simply because it doesn't require them to speak. Many marry the first person who comes along and accepts their speech disorder, rather than hold out for the love of their life. Many limit themselves to virtual friends on the Internet rather than seeking socialization within their own communities.

During the evening hours of those final seven days, the therapists force their patients onto the dreaded telephone. Each patient sits in a cubicle and for three hours every evening, scans over the classified ads in the newspaper and calls about the puppies for sale, or inquires as to what time the garage sale begins the next morning. On the final evening, the patients go to the local shopping mall as a group, and the therapists asks each patient to approach a shopper in the mall to ask what time it was. They would have the patients speak to retail clerks and ask questions about various products. This game went on for three hours up until the mall closed, at which point all of us returned to our hotel rooms and reflected on what had transpired that evening.

The following morning, the head therapist gathered us together in a room and asked us about our experiences at the mall. A hand shot up from the back of the room. The hand belonged to a man named Tom. We all gazed at Tom, shocked that he had volunteered so eagerly to share. Tom had been virtually silent the entire duration of the program. He was about 50 years old and was a big guy, but his silence and lack of involvement made him virtually invisible despite his stature.

Tom said that when he got back to the hotel, he sat on

the edge of the bed and began replaying everything that had just occurred. He then told us he began to cry, although I imagine sobbing is a better description. I am sure that it was more than a few casual tears that were released after fifty years of isolation.

"Why were you crying?" asked the therapist.

"Because last night, was the first night in my life, that I had ever spoken to a stranger," answered Tom. "I realized that I didn't want to be cooped up in my hotel room the rest of the night, I wanted to be back at the mall, talking to whoever was willing to listen to me."

We all started crying, even the macho high school quarterback who was going through the program along with us. I can only imagine the triumph and exhilaration that Tom had felt that night, coupled with the realization of how much he had missed out on all of those many years.

We all went our separate ways that afternoon. I have read that many people arrive home and immediately set about remolding their lives thanks to their sudden transformation. Some of them immediately quit the jobs that they've despised all these years. Some of them began flirting with members of the opposite sex for the first time in their lives, sometimes to the detriment of their marriages. Nearly all of them become more involved in their church or social organizations and I'm sure that virtually all of them are able to finally rid themselves of the fretfulness and apprehension that occurred every time they opened their mouths to speak.

I wish I had stayed in touch with Tom. I would love to

know what became of him and what he was able to later accomplish. The fact that Tom enrolled himself tells me that he felt that Someday he would talk to a stranger. In order to do so, he had to overcome enormous obstacles and conquer learned fears that had coagulated his every thought.

Imagine living your entire life without speaking to a stranger. Imagine overhearing a conversation near you that you long to be a part of but instead sit in silence. Visualize yourself experiencing a "love at first sight" moment and doing nothing to act on that impulse. Envision yourself spending thirty years in a cubicle doing a job you hate simply because of your fear of speaking.

Simply imagine the constant fear that Tom and so many like him lived with every day, a fear that dictated their agenda every day, a fear that they let deny them the simple joys and experiences that we all take for granted. And now realize the fact that he overcame those fears. He did what it took to make his Someday a reality. He did it, and because he could do it, YOU can too.

It Starts with Setting a Date

Evan: You knew it all along, didn't you? You knew the dam was unstable. If it hadn't been for the ark, my family, the neighbors... I fought you every step of the way.
God: Yes, but you did it.
Evan: So you had nothing to do with the flood? Like where the ark landed exactly?
God: I gave you a little shove at the end. Sue me. You did good, son. You changed the world.
Evan: No. No I didn't.
God: Well let's see. Spending time with your family making them very happy. You gave that dog a home.

- *Steve Carell and Morgan Freeman in "Evan Almighty*

What is the first thing a couple does after the guy proposes to the girl he wants to marry and she accepts?

They set a date on the calendar for the big event. They set a date because nothing gets done until a date is set. They can't reserve the church, book the florist, decide on a caterer, or pick their honeymoon destination until a date has been set. Once the date is set, the wheels can start moving. As each day gets marked off the calendar, the excitement and energy builds until the magical day when it all comes together. And why does a wedding come together in the end?

Because someone took action – the guy made his proposal, the girl accepted it, and together they set a date. Setting a date is critical. Try booking a photographer or a band without a date. They all require that you give them one, because without one, talking about a wedding is just that, talk. They don't manage their business around talk or else they would be out of business. Once a date is set, you can begin building your coalition of professionals that will make your wedding spectacular.

Years ago I was a classroom instructor at an Information Technology Certification school. I taught the curriculum for a high level Microsoft certification. IT Certification tests aren't like college midterms or finals. There is no prescribed date for the exam. You contact a testing center and book the exam at your convenience.

During the final two weeks of the course, I would ask the students when they were planning on taking the exam. Too often I would hear students say "I'm going to study and then take it when I feel I'm ready." I would always cringe when they said that. Experience told me that eighty percent of the time, those who said that never took the exam, because they were never ready. They were never ready, because they always put off studying, because after all, there wasn't a date set. Why worry about it if there isn't a date set?

If a date isn't set, there isn't a strong sense of urgency. If there's no urgency, it doesn't take long for procrastination to set in, and once procrastination sets in, inertia takes root, and once inertia takes root, nothing gets done. Nine months later, those same students would report that they hadn't taken the exam yet. Of course, by then the course was no longer fresh in their mind, and the thousands of dollars they spent, and the time they took out of their schedules to be in class was all for naught.

Which is why on the first day of class, I would begin instructing my students on how to go about taking the exam in a timely manner. It was a simple three word strategy, "set a date." I would tell the class to take out their calendar and count thirty days ahead from the final day of class and to mark that date as the exam date. I would then urge them to book their exam date online right there in class with their credit card so that everything was set. IT Certification exam fees are non-refundable so you can't get your money back if you never take the exam.

Of course, the students would ask, "What if I'm not ready to take the exam by then?"

My answer was simple. "Take it anyway."

"But the test costs a hundred dollars," they would respond. "What if I fail?"

"Then that is your punishment for not being prepared," I would answer. "Make sure you are ready by then. You have the knowledge. You have the desire. Now make it happen."

If the football team isn't prepared for this weekend's game, they still have to play, and as a result, they may get walloped, but the pain and humiliation of getting walloped will motivate them to be better prepared the next time.

There is another facet to setting the date. Tell as many people about this date as you can. A football team doesn't like to be blown out, especially in front of a crowd of tens of thousands of people, or in front of millions on network television. By publicizing your date to everyone around, you are adding an element of outside pressure to keeping a commitment to that date. You don't want your friends to think you backed out, do you? You don't want them to think you are a quitter or that you chickened out do you? Of course not.

Of course, not all of my students would book the date on that first day of class, but nearly everyone who did passed the course. Those who booked it also took the class more seriously and got more out of it. They asked more questions and stayed after class to obtain further information from me or elaborate more on a topic they were having trouble with. Imagine that.

Want to go on that dream vacation to Europe? Pick a date and buy a plane ticket right now. Yes, you might not get the best price today, but you'll have a date, you'll have a ticket, and you'll have the motivation to see it through. And when your friends are back at home still talking about their Somedays, you'll be atop the Eifel Tower gazing down at the streets of Paris. You'll be living your dream.

Want to finally quit your job. Pick a date and begin getting your finances in order. Let all of your friends know when your last day is going to be so that they can help you get the word out about your new business so that you'll be forced to stick to it, or face the humiliation of backing out.

Are you feeling the energy now? Are you feeling motivated? Then quick get your calendar and assign your Someday to an actual day. Sweep off the cobwebs of inertia and send procrastination packing, never to return again. Your Someday is now going to happen because you have a date.

Father Time Waits for No One

"Chasing dreams and racing father time."

- Kid Rock, Born Free

When you think of Father Time, one thinks of the old man with a scythe. He seems harmless. He looks and shuffles across the floor like a feeble old man. We look at him and feel little or no intimidation from him. We feel that we can outmaneuver his every move and stay step ahead of him. We think that we can ignore him until we are of old age.

There's one problem, Father Time drives a sports car.

To compound the problem, he upgrades to a faster model every year until one day he is driving a Lamborghini or an Aston Martin. By your 50's and 60's time is flying by so fast, you wonder where the years went when looking back?

Father Time doesn't look back though. He only looks towards the road ahead, his lead foot pressing the gas pedal harder upon each mile.

We often feel like we can make a deal with Father Time. We say stuff like:

"The holiday season is coming up so I will start dieting and exercising after New Year's."

"I'll take that rafting trip through the Grand Canyon after I retire from my career."

And so another three months pass by or another year or decade, and we think we've pulled one on Father Time. Everything seems perfectly okay in our life despite our procrastination. We think we pulled one on the old man.

Don't kid yourself and let the grass grow under your feet. Father Time is the master poker player because he holds all the cards. It may not seem like he has a hand that can beat yours, but he is only bluffing. He always has a royal flush and at some point he will call "All in" and take out your pair of Kings that you are feeling so confident about. The game is stacked against you. It's no different than Vegas, the longer you play, the more inevitable it is you are going to lose.

We'll heard the generic story about the man who worked so hard his whole life, putting off his dreams of enjoyment until retirement. Finally, one day he retires and heads to his favorite lake. He puts that new bass boat he had always wanted into the water and takes off to where he believes the fish are waiting for him. As he arrives at what he thinks is the perfect spot, the sun begins to rise over the horizon, creating a morning glow that shimmers across the water. He takes out that new rod and reel and draws it back to cast.

And then he grabs his chest and keels over.

Time is up, and Father Time just showed his royal flush.

Death is the ultimate example of running out of time,

but we can run out of time in many ways. There are many things we may want to do which require our bodies to be fit and our minds to be sharp. Most importantly though, we run out of time because many of the things we keep putting off involve others, and the clock is running for them too.

Maybe you want to spend more time with your kids now while they are young and eager to be with you. Maybe you keep putting off asking the girl you love for her hand in marriage despite her suggestive hints. Maybe you keep postponing that father-son trip to which your dad is constantly alluding.

What if years down the road you finally find the time years from now to be with your kids more? The problem is that by then, your kids may be in the next phase of their development and being with you isn't cool anymore. Those hugs and giggles that they were willing to dole out continuously to you when you couldn't make the time are no longer offered. In addition, your kids are more impressionable when they are young and as time goes on, your wisdom and guidance have less influence. When it comes to your kids, there will never be a more opportune time than right now to spend time with them.

What if you finally get up the nerve to propose to your girlfriend, but before you can open your mouth, she tells you that she has given up on you and found someone else, or she accepted a job opportunity in another part of the country. You feel your heart skip a beat, just as it skipped a beat the first time you met her. But this time, it skipped not out of romance, but out of pain. It hits you that the love of your life is leaving you forever.

What if when you finally decide to take your dad on that trip, you find out it's too late? Dementia has set in by now, and the best of him is gone. He can't quite remember when he wanted to take that father-son trip in the first place, or why, since it seems he has trouble recognizing you at all.

The truth is, while you may decide to wait, the world doesn't for you, because Father Time waits for no one. Time is your most precious commodity. You can make more money. You can even hire a plastic surgeon to make you look younger, but you can't obtain more time, not for you, nor those around you that you love. Like the opening to the infamous television documentary show, 60 Minutes, time is ticking, every minute, every hour, every day, and every year.

But one day you won't hear the ticking of the clock because it will be drowned out by a much louder noise, the sound of a sports car, a sports car driven by Father Time.

But don't listen for the roar of his engine. You can't control the day of his arrival anyway. Instead, go pursue what you are missing out on in life and seize the day, not just any day, your Someday!

You're Halfway There Believe it or Not

"Whoa, we're half way there, whoa, livin' on a prayer
Won't you take my hand and we'll make it I swear
Whoa, livin' on a prayer"

- Bon Jovi, *Livin on a Prayer*

You have a dream. Yes, maybe you spend a lot more time talking about your dream than you spend actually doing something to make it come true, but at least you have one. You have a goal, an objective, something to work toward, and something to hope for. You have a vision, an idea, an aspiration. You know what your destination is, and therefore, you know which direction you need to take to arrive there. You have some sense of the initial steps you must take. All you need is a little motivation, a little shove to get you going. Just like a rolling stone, once you start moving, each step towards your goal gets easier and easier.

It may seem like a long journey lies ahead of you. The obstacles that separate you from your dream may seem daunting. But here's the good news: No matter how lofty your dream may be, and no matter how long your journey, even though you haven't taken a single step . . .

You're halfway there! You are halfway to Someday!

How you might ask?

Because knowing where you want to go, and where you want to end up, is half the journey.

Because you have a Someday to strive toward, you don't have to use words like: what, why and where. You won't be continually asking questions such as:

- What do I want to do with my life when I am older?
- Why do I want to do such and such?
- Where do I want to go one day?

On the contrary, you will be opening your questions with the word, how, as you ask yourself:

- How do I get where I want to be?
- How do I go about accomplishing that?
- How will I feel when I achieve my goal?

When you have a dream, there's less uncertainty in your life, and fewer questions to ask.

Speaking of questions, have you ever met someone who didn't have a dream?

In the 1985 movie, Mask, a teenage boy named Rocky Dennis suffers from a skull deformity that causes him to look like a freak. Despite the hardship of dealing with the torment, pity and awkwardness doled out by humanity, Rocky goes through life with a wonderful attitude, thanks to a dedicated mom and her biker gang. Their collective love for Rocky, and Rocky's dream to travel throughout Europe, keeps him going each and every day. Rocky keeps a map of the region in his room with a pin inserted on every European city that he yearns to see. Every time he reads about, or hears about, a new city, he inserts a new pin onto the map.

At the end of the movie, his dream of motorbike trip through Europe collapses when his best friend, Ben, who was to come with him tells him that he is moving back to Michigan for good. . Afterwards, fighting a fierce headache he quietly withdraws to his room, removes the tacks from his map of Europe, and goes to bed, and during the night dies in his sleep. Without his dream, he had no reason to go on living.

I often discuss this idea of not having a dream with a relative of mine who is now in his mid-70's. After retiring from an active career, he finds himself sitting with his computers in his dimly lit basement each and every day. He attempts to play the stock market as a day trader. It is more an endeavor to pass the time than a means to make money. He doesn't know what to do with himself at this point in his life. He has no dreams.

"Why don't you do some volunteer work? There are surely many organizations who would value your vast experience and skills," I propose to him.

"Well what if I don't like it?" he responds to me."

"Then you will quit and look for the next thing," I answer.

'Well I don't know what type of organization I would want to work for."

"Well then, maybe get a job at Wal-Mart as a greeter and say hello to people three days a week. You know what that entails."

"But I don't know what I want to do."

"Well do something," I plead.

One day, I told him my story of meeting a retired corporate vice president who works at a private golf course as a starter (a starter is the person who greets the golfers at the first tee). This gentleman had shared with me how much joy it brings him. I asked my relative how he felt about becoming a starter since he used to be an avid golfer.

"I can't believe a corporate vice president would work as a starter for ten dollars an hour," he retorted. "Why would he do that?"

"Because he's not doing it for the money! He enjoys spending his days in a beautiful setting and conversing with other men who share his love of golf. Yes, he had a high paying job throughout his entire career, and yet, his Someday may always have been to work at a golf course, in an environment he truly loves. Maybe, he's finally doing what he always dreamed of doing, but couldn't."

One of the ladies I work with has a husband who spends every weekend working from home on his laptop. He doesn't have to work, but he doesn't know what else to do with his free time. He doesn't have a dream.

Without a dream, you lack a guiding force to navigate you through life. Without a dream, one is like a fish out of water, flopping on the beach with no sense of direction.

For example, this woman's husband works every weekend, not because his job demands it, but because he doesn't have a clue about what else to do.

Not everyone has a Someday to reach for. Not everyone has that captivating oasis just beyond the horizon to point toward. Not everyone has that mental imagery of accomplishment and celebration that allows him or her to escape the turmoil of a bad day.

Those without a dream are wanderers. But you *have* a dream! You *have* the Someday that is your navigational beacon. It is the X on your treasure map. You know where you are now, and you know where you want to be.

You are half way there!

A Wish Isn't the Same as a Dream

"I'm gonna dream you right into my life."

-   Cliff Richard, *Dreamin'*

We all know the famous "I Have a Dream Speech" delivered by Martin Luther King Jr. in Washington D.C. on August 28, 1963. It is a powerful speech, one that evokes great emotion and passion. It is a speech that moves the human spirit and inspires men to march together as one to right an injustice. It is a speech that once delivered, promised to change the course of history. It is a speech with a message of immortality that will connect with generations a thousand years from now.

Notice that Rev. King used the word dream and not wish. A wish is not a dream. A dream is something we strive for. A dream is something we deem obtainable. It is something we feel we can achieve on our own. A dream is something that motivates us to overcome great impediments. A dream gives us hope for a brighter tomorrow. A dream encourages us through the long and difficult journey and helps keep us focused on the end game. A dream arouses our spirits even in the most troubling of times. A dream is a reality we hope to accomplish or achieve.

A dream is something we can believe in.

A wish is a very different matter. We associate a wish with a genie, some fantastical being that lives inside a magic lamp. A genie is a fairy tale, willing to call us "Master" and serve us, granting us three wishes no matter how outlandish they may seem. A wish is something that is "a one in a million." A wish is a long shot. A wish is something that we can only achieve by crossing our fingers. A wish is a fairy tale, if even that.

A dream, is something of substance, something worth fighting for. Take the Rev. King's speech for example:

"I have a dream that my four little children will one day live in a nation where they will not be judged by the color of their skin but by the content of their character. I have a dream today!"

A dream is something we feel we can reach if only given a little more time. It is something that lies just beyond our grasp. It is an endpoint we feel we can reach with just a series of management-calculated steps.

A wish is about winning a million dollars that we've never worked for. A wish is a handsome movie star she's never met asking her to marry him. A wish will magically transport us into a new life, defying the basic laws of time and space.

A dream is something we plan for in order to accomplish it. A dream is something we witness realizing before our eyes, piece by piece.

A wish is the quarterback throwing the fifty yard bomb of desperation on his back foot as he is tackled to the ground. A wish is putting a dollar down on five numbers at the local convenience store to win the lottery.

A dream is something we curse ourselves for if we don't reach out for it.

A wish is something we shrug our shoulders about if we neglect to ask for it.

A dream is something that saddens us if we never see it come to fruition. A wish is something we never really counted on anyway. We don't buy a lottery ticket because we honestly believe we are going to win. We buy a lottery ticket so we don't feel guilty for not buying one.

Do you see the difference between these two now? Do you recognize the weakness of using the phrase "I wish?" It's not a deadly phrase like "I should," is but compared to a dream a wish is frail and tired. It calls for no action on your part. Compare the phrases below.

I dream of quitting this dead end job and starting my own business one day.

I wish I didn't work here and that I could start my own business.

See how the word dream is a forward-thrusting statement. It is an idea that deals with the present and the future. The word "could" is many times used in an "I wish" statement. The dictionary defines the word could as: "a word used to indicate ability or permission in the past." This makes a wish even weaker, as we all know you can't change the past.

How about these two contrasting statements:

- I dream of going to Europe one day.

- I wish I could go to Europe one day.

There is the word "could" again. See how the first statement sounds like a statement of faith and empowerment while the second statement sounds like a faint act of requesting permission, as if you were asking the teacher to let you out of the corner.

We don't need a genie to see our Somedays come to fruition. The beauty of desiring to quit that dead end job is that you alone have the ability to make it a reality. You can quit that job tomorrow if you really want to.

"But what about my bills?" you ask. "I just can't quit my job and still pay my bills."

Well then, get rid of that new car you purchased a year ago and replace it with a much older practical model. Stop going out to eat and stock up on macaroni and cheese. Don't plan any vacations for a while and cancel that expensive cable TV subscription. Get your finances in order and then make the jump.

"But I can't do all of that," you retort. "I have to retain my current lifestyle."

Well in that case, you do need a genie, for there's no way to make a dramatic change in your life without the dominoes falling in other aspects. Yes, you can't quit a job, without tightening your belt, while you struggle through the transition of recalibrating your life.

Dreams are worth making sacrifices. Dreams are worth the toil, the labor and the foregoing of immediate gratification. A wish is simply worth a few spare coins tossed into some fountain.

Is your Someday worth more than some spare change in your pocket?

Then pronounce your Someday in the form of a dream, an obtainable dream that you, and only you, can attain.

The Curse of Being Capricorn

Wendy let me in I wanna be your friend
I want to guard your dreams and visions
Just wrap your legs round these velvet rims
And strap your hands across my engines
Together we could break this trap
We'll run till we drop, baby we'll never go back
Will you walk with me out on the wire
`cause baby I'm just a scared and lonely rider
But I gotta find out how it feels
I want to know if love is wild, girl I want to know if
love is real

- Bruce Springsteen, *Born To Run*

I am a Capricorn. I've never been one to look at my daily astrology chart, but my dad instilled a sense of Capricorn pride in me from an early age. My dad is a Capricorn as well. He told me he even had a boss at one time who only hired Capricorns. If you are unfamiliar with the Capricorn symbolism, we are the mountain goat that scales the rocky cliffs. We are planners and are constantly working on multiple goals simultaneously. Like a good chess player, we are always thinking five moves ahead. We are part juggler and part conjurer, part manager and part engineer. We need our lives to be in order to keep everything running smoothly.

We relentlessly pursue our goals and do not rest until we achieve our objectives. Everything we do is about reaching the end goal. We are obsessed with seeing the fruition of our dreams. Almost everything we do is part of a greater plan. Every act, every intention, every undertaking has a purpose.

We are silent achievers, and most people underestimate us. They compare us in contrast to the robust looking Aries ram, Taurus the bull or Leo the lion and just nod their heads. They say to themselves that goat doesn't have a chance.

But while those mighty signs charge ahead of us, relying on their physical strength to overcome whatever obstacles lie ahead, we have already mapped out the journey. And as they stumble, and eventually fall, tumbling back down the mountain, we meticulously make our way up the rocky cliffs, one step at a time, carefully maneuvering the narrow path, until finally it is us who stand at the crest of the mountain peak, enjoying the view in our success and triumph. Never underestimate the goat.

Being a Capricorn is also a curse. For as we are enjoying the crisp mountain air, the wondrous view from the mountain peak we have just scaled, taking in the sense of accomplishment, we see another mountain peak just ahead. That mountain is taller than the one where we stand, its view even more enticing, or so we tell ourselves. This discovery propels us forward on an endless journey to scale that next peak, and the next one, and the next, for there is always another one. Any sense of accomplishment is quickly circumvented by the desire to achieve the next objective. It is a never-ending cycle. It is the curse of the Capricorn.

It gets tiring being the goat. Ask those who personally know us well, and they will tell you. Now and then, we crash from exhaustion. At times we get overwhelmed from overcommitting ourselves. We forget that Father Time only allots 24 hours in a day, and that we have to find time to sleep at some point. However, it's hard to sleep restfully on the mountain. There is nowhere soft to rest your head, the air is cold, and you have to constantly be aware of the edge of the cliff beside you.

Lately, I have taken a break now and then, while ascending whichever mountain I happen to be climbing at the time, and gaze down at the lush green meadow below me. The problem with climbing rocky cliffs is having to constantly watch out for the trail in front of you, a trail of dirt, gravel and an occasional boulder. The sprouts of grass growing along those cliffs are few and far between and barely satisfy. I have recently become infatuated with the meadow below and long to repose in its appealing dark green blades of grass. The meadow looks so inviting. I long to run amongst the blooming wildflowers and enjoy their fragrant smells. I aspire to enjoy the warmth of the sunshine, rather than continue to endure the cold thin air of the mountains. I dream of spending days upon days in the meadow with no sense of purpose other than my own personal enjoyment and pleasure. Rather than accomplish lofty dreams of aspiration, I find myself desiring only to lie in the meadow on a comfortable blanket with the woman I love beside me as we bask in the sun, relishing the simple enjoyments in life we've missed.

The truth is, I am tired of climbing mountains. I now long for the simple pleasures of life. My definition of Someday has now changed.

Earlier in my life I said, "Someday, I am going to record an album," and I did.

Earlier in my life I said, "Someday, I am going to become a syndicated newspaper columnist," and I did.

Earlier in my life I said, "Someday, I am going to break into the IT field and be very successful despite no formal academic IT training," and I did.

Earlier in my life I said, "Someday, I am going to run for political office and get elected," and I did.

Earlier in my life I said, "Someday, I am going to write a book," and I did.

But now I want something completely different.

I accomplished so much in my life thus far, and yet I felt unhappy. I sought a counselor last year to help me examine my life. During our first two sessions, she asked me a number of questions about all of the commitments in my life at the time. At the end of the second session she said, "As I look over my notes at everything you've told me about your life right now, the word that comes to my mind is OVERWHELMING! Where is your fun? Where is your night out with the boys to go bowling, or play poker, or do a round of golf on a Saturday? You have to crash at some point. There's no way you can keep up this pace without a breakdown now and then. How have you managed to keep going at this pace for so long?"

She was right. There was little fun in my life. That was the moment I realized that I was tired of constantly climbing. What good is accomplishing greatness if I have no time to enjoy it? On my deathbed one day, it is not my accomplishments that I will relish in my last moments of life, but the loving and joyful memories that I created at one time or another with the people I love.

As I walked out of her office, I said to myself, "Someday I am going to do nothing, nothing but enjoy life to its fullest."

Yes, Someday, I am going to put the needs of my heart above the needs of my financial obligations. Someday, I am going to put my personal needs ahead of my career. Someday I am going to rediscover my spirituality. Someday I am going to wake up and spend the entire day with the woman I love beneath the sheets. Someday, I am going to enjoy doing nothing.

Doing nothing is very hard for a mountain goat. It's not in our nature. But I know that if I don't attain my Someday now, that I may never see it come to fruition until it's too late to fully enjoy it. It was upon leaving her office that the idea for this book came to fruition. I also realized something else that day. I recognized that I am 49 years old and that it is a very critical year for me as a human being, which is what the next chapter is all about.

Remember your 20's?

In another life, I would be your girl
We keep all our promises, be us against the world
In another life I would make you stay
So I don't have to say, you were the one that got away

   -Katie Perry, *The One that Got Away*

Ah, your 20's.

It was the time when you had your whole life ahead of you. You had your youth and your dreams. You were armed with an endless abundance of energy, potential and optimism and felt there was nothing you couldn't do. It was a magical time.

At the start of your 20's, you were probably working on completing your education. Maybe you were wrapping up your associates degree or vocational studies. Maybe you had finally gotten to your core classes, while working towards your four year degree, thinking that you were finally tapping the knowledge base you needed to jumpstart your career. At some point, you completed your education, and by fulfilling your certificate or degree requirements, you relinquished the final anchor that was tying you down to any person, or to any particular place. You could now go anywhere. You were free of your parents, free of your professors and free of your school mandates.

Perhaps, higher education was never your goal, and after high school you went straight into the work force, learning how to work with others while acquiring lifelong work skills and habits. Maybe you had the aspiration to start your own business venture and be your own boss. You desired freedom, and freedom you had. You just didn't appreciate it back then.

No matter which path you chose, at some point in your early 20's, you became beholden to no one. You were devoid of obligations or commitments. You could choose whatever path you wanted and go where ever your dreams took you. You had few responsibilities, other than maybe a part-time job. You had no financial commitments other than a small credit card balance, a car payment or a student loan that had to be paid at some point. Whatever your financial obligations, they were negligible and manageable.

You were so young, with all the time in the world in front of you. There were a million paths you could have taken and thousands of thrilling adventures you could have experienced. You could have:

- Backpacked across Europe

- Lived at the beach, enjoying the sand by day and working tables at night for tips

- Written a book to see if you could make a living as an author

- Perfected a musical instrument and jammed with other budding musicians

- Tried at hand at a number of career paths to see what worked best

- Dated lots of interesting people before settling down later in life

There were an infinite number of things you could have done. But like most people in their 20's, you made a critical mistake and squandered those years, failing to take advantage of them.

So what was the mistake you made?

You didn't realize a simple truth.

You only get ten years in your 20's.

Because before you knew it, you were in your 30's.

And your 30's are nothing like your 20's. In your 30's, you begin planting roots and taking on adult responsibility. By age 30, you've probably married someone and the two of you are anticipating your first child, about to learn the sacrifices that come with raising children. You have probably closed on your first house by now, and besides saddling yourself with a mortgage, you discover all of the other costs of home ownership such as: property taxes, utilities, repairs, upgrades, and insurance. It is during this time that you begin making an impact in your career field, but you're still at the low end of the totem pole. Therefore, you have to hustle and perform the endless tasks that tend to get foisted on the guys at the lower layers of the pyramid. Don't get me wrong. It's a magical time. It's the time for framing your future, rather than just working on the foundation you built up to that point. It's a wonderful period of life. It's just all about the family unit throughout your thirties. It's not a time to be selfish because it's not about you.

During these years, your weekends consist of carting your kids to birthday parties and soccer games. While summer meant a gamut of endless opportunities in your 20's, you're pretty much locked into going to Disney World for summer vacation, or seeing the grandparents to show off how much the kids have grown since the last visit. Between the demands of kids, your spouse and your boss, your 30's are pretty much on auto-pilot. At this point, life directs you, rather than you directing life.

And then come your 40's. It's a decade of real maturity. You have twenty years of experience now as an adult, and you have accumulated the wisdom to match. You realize you've made some mistakes due to immaturity in the past, but you've learned from them. You make wiser decisions now than you used to. If you made smart choices in your 20's and 30's, you're starting to enjoy some of the benefits of those decisions. You're starting to see your life come together during these years.

You're also starting to witness the signs that you're not as young as you used to be. You gain weight a lot easier than you did ten years ago, and it's a lot harder to lose it. Your son can outrun you, and your kids seem to catch on to new technology and new trends much faster than you.

Speaking of your kids, they are in middle school now and they are starting to rebel. They don't seem to want to hang out with you as much anymore. You're not as cool as you once were. While you used to pray for a few minutes of silence in the house after a hard day at work, now you beg them to give you more than just those few customary phrases they constantly dole out like "Nothing" and "I don't know."

You've finally broken through the glass ceiling at work, and your career is starting to take shape. You're in management now, and although the paycheck is bigger, so are the responsibilities, which brings on greater stress in your life. Work seems to consume even more of your energy now.

This is the decade where you start to accumulate a lot of stuff. You're probably in your second house as your family outgrew the first one. This one gives you more room for the kids and a home office for you or your spouse, but it also comes with a bigger mortgage payment. There seems to be some home improvement project to tackle every weekend. This is when you start buying those expensive toys you've always wanted, and no matter how big the house is, it seems there is never enough storage to host all of your possessions.

It's a time of inner reflection as you see the flashing sign ahead that says, "Middle Age." You start imagining what you will want to do if and when you are able to retire. You begin to retrace your footsteps in order to reexamine how you got to where you are today, and where you went wrong. It's a time of self-appraisal, as we start to ask ourselves if we are truly happy, or dare to even ask the question, "What really makes us happy?"

The 40's decade is when we start to daydream and start talking about Someday.

But here's the good news, your 50's are coming, and your 50's are like your 20's.

Don't believe me?

Your 20's were special because you were finally out of the house and away from your parents. Well how old were your parents when you got out of the house?

They were in their 50's.

So they got to be rid of you too, and soon, you will be rid of your kids, and then, just like in your 20's, you will be able to selfishly devote most of your attention to yourself. You will have freedom again.

Your new "empty nester" status means you don't need all those extra bedrooms and bathrooms now, nor the finished basement. You can scale down, and since you don't have to concern yourself with schools, you can move anywhere you want.

The fact that you're scaling down means that your mortgage will be less, as well as all the utilities and other pesky bills that come along with home ownership. You're also spending less on food and necessities with less mouths to feed. All in all, you've got less money leaving your checking account each month, which means you don't need to bring in as much either if you wish.

In your 50's, you're at the height of your career. You are peaking now in productivity and efficiency at work. Between your reduced financial responsibilities and your high potency job performance, you won't need to spend as much time on the job, which means more time to apply to the things you love.

Just about whatever your Someday is, your 50's is a wonderful time to pursue it. Because of your newfound freedom, you are able to:

- Travel to all those amazing places you have always dreamed of
- Part ways with your spouse and begin your journey to find your soul mate if you wish

- Spend more time with friends, or make new ones as you frequent those cafes and restaurants you have time to visit now

Because you don't have to work as much due to reduced expenditures and increased productivity, you will have more time to:

- Work on your book idea and publish it

- Get in shape and promote a healthier lifestyle

- Buy that bike you've always wanted to ride on Route 66, or on those meandering mountain roads you love

You see, all of the elements have come together that you enjoyed in your 20's. You have more freedom, less commitments and more time. True, you aren't as young and limber as you were in your 20's, but unlike those younger years, you have money this time, and money has a way of compensating for that to some extent.

And this time you have one other key asset in your arsenal: wisdom.

In your '50's, you now know what you failed to realize back in your 20's. You only get ten of these years.

Because your 60's aren't like your 50's. In your 60's, your body does indeed begin slowing down more. You don't have the stamina you had in your 50's. It's also when you start seriously looking at retirement, which puts you in more of a hibernation mode. It's not a time to take risks.

And one thing you can't risk happening is to not to see your Someday come true.

But you get another bite at the apple!

Because you get to relive your 20's again, thirty years later.

You're Only Young Once

May the good Lord be with you down every road you roam.
And may sunshine and happiness surround you when you're far from home.
And may you grow to be proud, dignified and true.
And do unto others as you'd have done to you.
Be courageous and be brave.
And in my heart you'll always stay
Forever Young.

    -Rod Stewart, *Forever Young*

Maybe you are in your late teens or early to mid-20's, and you just read the previous chapter and are saying, "I'm not in my 50s so how does this book apply to me? I barely use the word Someday because I'm not really sure what I want to do with my life yet."

Which is great! Think about the Somedays often recited by people in their 40's and 50's.. They want to quit that job they hate and do something they truly enjoy. They want to finally lose weight and get in shape. They want to get out of their massive debt and live a simpler life. They want to leave a bad marriage and find true love.

What do all of these Somedays have in common?

They all involve regret.

The dictionary defines regret as "a feeling of disappointment or distress about something that one wishes could be different."

The beautiful thing about the age you're at is that you can do it right the first time. You can escape the dejection of regret later in life. You can avoid the mistakes that most people make in their 20's. You can do it right the first time around.

We already covered the first mistake most of us make in our 20's, the failure to realize that your 20's only last for ten years. The other classic mistake that so many make during this period is that they place urgency around the wrong types of things:

- I need to hurry up and graduate so I can start my career

- I need to get a job quickly so I can start obtaining the things I want in life

- I need to buy a new car to show off my success

- I need to hurry up and find someone so that I can get married and have kids by age _____.

You get the picture. In our 20's, we place so much

urgency on jumping into a '30's mentality. You have the rest of your life to worry about a mortgage and kids. You have the rest of your life to figure out how to get out of your cubicle and move up to that corner office with the view. You have the rest of your life to buy a fancier car than the one in your neighbor's driveway. You have the rest of your life to worry about being responsible for other people.

Take advantage of your freedom and mobility at this early stage in life. You can pursue any path you want to right now.

There are things you can do now that are quite burdensome later in life. Take travel for instance. When college kids want to head to Florida for spring break, they simply pile into the most dependable vehicle among their group of friends and head down to a hotel of some sort. They aren't worried about what the hotel amenities are because they are going down there to experience the beach. It's all about having fun, getting too much sun while you drink too much alcohol and maybe luck out and find a hot guy or girl. The experience is everything.

Now examine how people with families in their '30's and '40's travel. They have to bring car seats to strap in the kids. It takes forever to get where they are going because they have to take regular pit stops for "potty breaks." They have to worry about whether or not they brought enough videos to keep the kids entertained. They also have firm expectations and demands about the type of room they want, which costs a lot more money, meaning they can't afford to stay as long to enjoy the beach.

See how easy things are when you are young? Life gets so complicated as the years go by. Think of all of the things you could do right now. Unless they require money, or a certain degree of knowledge and experience, it will never be easier to do those things than it is right now.

Because of your youthfulness, you are strong and robust, so don't be afraid to do things differently. Take college for instance. Parents, and society at large, tend to push young people into attending college. College is not for everyone, and it isn't right for all fields either. Yes, guidance counselors and politicians love to cite how college graduates earn so much more money over a lifetime than non-college graduates do. But here is a little secret. In a free market society, smart people who work efficiently and are creative to some degree get rewarded in life, and those are the types of people who tend to go to college. Going to college may be simply a common trait amongst successful people and nothing more.

I met a college student once who was majoring in photography because he wanted to be a photographer. What does a college degree have to do with being a photographer? In the end, the only thing that makes a difference in photography is the beauty and quality of the pictures you take. If you want to be a photographer, take a few photography classes and get an internship with an established photographer. Eventually, you will hone your craft and people will begin hiring you.

I met another young lady who was majoring in sports marketing because she wanted to work in the marketing department for a hockey team one day. She was going to school full time and working part time to help pay her expenses. I told her that instead of going to college, she should contact all of the minor league hockey teams across the country and talk her way into some type of job or internship for one of them. She would learn far more about what's required to work for a hockey team that way than she would by sitting in some stale college classroom. She would make lots of professional contacts and gain valuable knowledge and experience, which would allow her to work her way up the ladder. Sure, she wouldn't make much money in the beginning, but she would still end up further ahead financially than she would by doling out thousands of dollars on her college education

What's the hurry to go to college? There are hundreds of thousands of recent college graduates right now who thought that college was their magic ticket who are sitting at home unemployed. Instead of running off to college, why not go to Europe for six months while you're young and don't care if you stay in a four star hotel? Go and see the Eiffel tower, Big Ben or the Sistine Chapel. Do it while you're young! Or maybe go and live at the beach for a year, working as a life guard, a bartender or waitress. Just think of the experiences you could have! Those are the kinds of things you can only do when you are young. You have the rest of your life to do the "9 to 5 thing.

According to the National Center for Educational Statistics, the average annual cost for a student to go to school at a public university was just shy of $20,000, a private university nearly costing nearly $30,000. According to an article titled, "The Myth of the Four Year College Degree" in the January 10, 2013 edition of Time Magazine, only 53% of full-time college students graduate within six years. If we look at these figures, conservatively, let's take a five year graduation period at $20,000 per year. That comes to a cost of $100,000. Think of all those college graduates in their early to mid-20's who spent a hundred thousand dollars (or at least someone did) on that college education. But, in addition to that huge expenditure, they also paid a huge opportunity cost to go to college because they could have elected to work full-time during those years. Even if they only averaged ten dollars an hour over the course of that time period, it would amount to an additional $100,000. So that basic college education now cost them $200,000. Was it worth it? Could they have spent that money more effectively?

What if instead you had served as an apprentice for someone in a field that interested you and learned the ropes from them over that same four or five year period? Then, you could have borrowed that same

$200,000 and started your own business!

The truth is that by the time the majority of college graduates reach their '40's, they are working in a field that has nothing to do with their college degree. Most were never asked what their GPA was in college. In fact, looking back, they realize that what they did in college had little to do with the success attained in their careers. I, myself, look back wishing I had spent more time partying and loving life on a moment by moment basis in college since, what I studied in college has had almost nothing to do with the various careers I have had over the past fifteen years.

If you are in your 20's, vow to live this decade in such a manner that you will never say the words, "Someday I'm going to _____". Understand that you only get ten years in your 20's, and that there is no urgency to rush into the responsibilities of your '30's. Realize that your life is the simplest it will ever be right now so take advantage of that before life gets complicated. Know that you don't have to take the same road that everyone else is taking. Just because the majority is maneuvering down that path doesn't mean it is the road to success. Don't be afraid to take a risk and do something different than your peers or your family before you did.

But just in case you get your 20's perfect, go ahead and read the rest of the book.

Enjoying the Lush Opportunities Life has to Offer

"There is no security in this world, only opportunity."

-        General Douglas MacArthur

Opportunity is everywhere. We just have to recognize it when we see it. An opportunity is something we rarely plan for ahead of time. We just have to act on it when it comes our way. Many times, it is hard to recognize opportunity from far away. It is not until we become actively involved in the pursuit of our dreams that we discover opportunities that will take us where we want to be in a manner we never anticipated.

Years ago, at the start of my career, I had the good fortune to work for a wonderful boss named Herb. Herb was a care free spirit. He never stayed in any one place for very long. His career included a long list of employers who needed his knowledge about market research to help them better define and reach out to a product's target consumer. Although he frequently changed jobs, he always left every organization better than it was before he had arrived, something I have always strived to achieve myself.

As a young man, I was enthralled by his many stories

of accomplishments throughout his life, and I told him that I hoped to be as successful as he one day. I asked him for advice on how to plan my career as he had, for as I mentioned earlier, Capricorns are planners.

Herb was aware of my obsession with planning my future. "I was a planner too once," he said, "until the day a horse redefined my philosophy of life."

He then began to tell me about the day he went horseback riding, while living out in Montana in his younger days. He enjoyed riding horseback across the beautiful Montana wilderness, which I understand is simply breathtaking.

> "I had ridden my horse through the hills
> throughout the morning. I came across a lovely
> meadow that opened up before me. Both the
> horse and I were in need of a rest so I decided
> to dismount my horse and eat the lunch I had
> packed in my saddle bag. Rather than tie my
> horse, I decided to let it roam free and enjoy the
> nice green grass that the meadow boasted.
> Lunch for me resulted in a nap, and upon
> waking up, I anxiously glanced around for my
> four-legged companion. Not seeing him in the
> immediate area, I sprang to my feet and began
> nervously gazing across the meadow to locate
> him. And spot him I did, far off on the other
> side of the meadow, for I had been asleep for
> more than an hour. I brought my eyes back to
> his original location, where I had begun eating

my lunch, and I began tracing the steps of his journey across the meadow. It was easy to retrace his path simply by looking for the leaves of grass that he had nibbled down to the sheath, which formed a meandering trail that zigzagged all the way across the field." The path that he had taken appeared to have no rhyme or reason at first glance, but upon further examination, I recognized the beauty of the path taken by the horse, for it steered him to the lushest, greenest grass comprised within the meadow.

I thought to myself, if I had sought to get to the other side of the meadow, I would have simply taken the straightest, most logical course to get there. I would have arrived in the quickest amount of time, but would have missed out on the finer opportunities the meadow had to offer. The horse paid no attention to the other side of the meadow, but instead put his nose to the ground and let his sense of taste and smell guide him from one stretch of the finest grass to the next, eventually finding himself to the other side of the meadow anyway. Though he would have arrived much later, his journey was far more satisfying and rewarding, having experienced some of the best eating the meadow had to offer. It was at that moment that I decided that I would live my life like that horse. I wouldn't take the most apparent route from point A to point B, or the shortest one. I

*would put my nose to the ground and let my
instinct guide me. I vowed then to always
recognize the richest opportunities around me
and act on them, and like that horse, I would
always delight in the lushest pleasures and
greenest ventures of life. I have never
regretted that decision."*

Herb's story about the horse is a wonderful example of
how important it is to actively participate in life, and to
be conscious of opportunity when it unveils itself right
beneath our noses. Planning is important, but the
best-laid plans are only constructed by the information
immediately at hand. Armies go into battle based on a
plan, but they continually modify it, as holes and
weaknesses are discovered within enemy lines.
Football coaches make halftime adjustments based on
the performance of both teams on the field during the
first half of the football game.

The fact is that there are lush opportunities all around
us, ripe for the taking. Although we may know the final
destination we're headed toward, the most direct route
isn't necessarily the best one. Life is about
experiences. Often, we don't see the most gratifying
moments and valuable occurrences that happen to us
in life ahead of time. As Herb discovered that day in
the meadow, many times the prospect of being solely
transfixed on our destination on the other side of the
meadow can eclipse the string of opportunities that
would otherwise take us to the same place, more

nourished and fulfilled than if we had set a straight course for the horizon in the distance. It is a simple fact that a horse understands. Sometimes, we as humans need to avoid overthinking. We need to cease out-strategizing ourselves, and act on instinct. By modifying our best-laid plans, we ensure that we not only scale the mountain, but we enjoy the climb as well.

Each minute of life is precious. We must maximize each and every moment, and eat the finest grass in the meadow.

I Know Not Where the Birds have Gone

A little voice inside my head said, "don't look back,
you can never look back."
I thought I knew what love was
What did I know?
Those days are gone forever
I should just let them go but -- I can see you --
Your brown skin shining in the sun
I see you walking real slow and you're smiling at
everyone
I can tell you my love for you will still be strong
After the boys of summer have gone

-    Don Henley, Boys of Summer

Sometimes your Someday involves more than just yourself. Sometimes your Someday involves other people as well. If so, that is a huge responsibility because any procrastination on the part of one of you impacts the other's opportunity to see the fruition of your collective Someday. Let's say you are a woman who has been living with a guy for four or five years now and he still hasn't asked you to marry him, despite all of the conversations the two of you have had about getting married Someday. The truth is, without his proactive involvement, you are never going to get married no matter how committed you are to the goal and how much energy you are willing to put into seeing it through unless he does something as well. Sometimes, despite our best efforts, we just have to take our ball and go home.

This is a story about two people in love, Gus and Lisa. They both shared a dream. They both talked endlessly about their Someday when they would finally be together and live happily ever after. Gus was vigilant in seeing his Someday come to fruition. Gus wasn't willing to let anything stand in his way of attaining his dream. Unfortunately, the only thing that could stop his dreams of being with Lisa, was Lisa herself. Lisa was unwilling to do anything more than simply talk about their Someday together. The lesson of this story is simple. If you share a Someday with another person and you are a Lisa, you need to be honest with yourself. Are you truly willing to take the difficult steps necessary in order to attain your shared goal? If not, your reluctance to take action and keep putting it off until tomorrow isn't just holding you back, it is holding back the other party as well. This isn't fair to the other person. If you are a Gus, you need to not only take action yourself and stick to your date, but you have to enforce action with the person who shares your Someday as well. This of course is extremely difficult, for just as its easy for Lisa to keep convincing herself that "tomorrow" she will finally take that difficult step she keeps putting off, it is easy for Gus to keep convincing himself that "tomorrow" Lisa will indeed find the resolve to take that step.

Without further ado, here is the story of Gus and Lisa.

Gus served our country with pride during his years of military service. After leaving the military his decisions garnered him a degree of financial security. Gus has made many great decisions throughout his years and has accomplished much. However, few people are strong in all facets of their life, and unfortunately, his love life hasn't proved as successful.

Gus was married for 35 years. It was his wife's third marriage and she brought three kids into the matrimony as well. Gus took them in and helped raise them as if they were his own. Gus said it didn't take long to recognize a high degree of dissatisfaction in his marriage. His wife always seemed to be complaining about something, and soon the criticisms began outnumbering the 'I love you's.' Towards the end of his military career, Gus served in Iraq during Desert Storm in 1990. Gus divulged to me that while other soldiers serving in Iraq received letters in perfumed envelopes full of romantic declarations of love, the letters he received were riddled with grumblings and grievances about his wife's life and how it was all his fault.

Things only got worse when he returned home. Her badgering became a part of the daily routine of life for him. While those around him recognized his achievements and successes, she only belittled him with disparaging remarks. There was little joy in Gus's life when he was home, which is why he readily accepted a promising opportunity in another city. It was a management position which would compensate him very well, a fact that his wife was very much in favor of. It would also provide him some unique challenges that would engulf a lot of his focus and attention, giving him an excuse to be away from his abhorrent domestic environment. He was looking forward to getting lost in his work.

Upon his arrival, Gus found something even greater to get lost in, a fellow employee named Lisa. When you're in a horrible marriage full of strife and verbal abuse, it's easy to hide it from your neighbors, colleagues and even family if you only see them during holidays now and then. You can't hide it from other people in similarly unhappy marriages. They easily see through the façade. When they meet you they can detect the lonesome spirit inside of you. They know what the lie looks like as they too are living it. Gus and Lisa recognized this about each other right from the start. In addition to being able to relate to her marital life, Gus found Lisa to be drop dead gorgeous. For him it was love at first sight.

Lisa's husband was very controlling and kept her at bay through an endless bombardment of verbal abuse. It's truly amazing how many gorgeous women there are out there who are completely insecure about themselves due to years of being put down by their husbands. Lisa, like many women in similar circumstances, appeared vivacious and effervescent on the outside, but inside she lacked confidence and self-esteem.

"I immediately felt a zeal to expose her to life much more than she was accustomed," said Gus. "We started out with some very enjoyable and lengthy lunches. We both had a lot of freedom at work. Soon our lunches led to us traveling together on business trips, sometimes of a week-long duration. We went to Tampa Bay, the California Coast, Dallas and Saint Louis just to name a few. We enjoyed experiencing those things together in each new city we visited. It was such a wonderful time and a true escape from our decrepit home lives."

Gus is a true gentleman and refused to disclose any of the intimate details of his affair with Lisa. He did tell me how strong he felt when she was in his arms. Her love for him gave him a sense of confidence that he had been lacking for decades, a confidence that gave him the strength to finally file for divorce. "I knew I had to leave at that point," interjected Gus, "as I only had a couple ounces of pride left in me by then."

Not surprisingly, his wife dragged out their divorce proceedings for as long as possible, milking the situation for as long as she legally could. Finally, three years into their affair, it was over. He was free, legally and morally, to love any woman in the world of his choosing. There was only one woman however that he had any interest in loving, and that was Lisa.

Like Gus, Lisa spoke constantly about leaving her spouse one day and running off together. She also expressed a lot of fears about leaving her husband. "My friends told me I was crazy to wait around for her," said Gus. "They told me that there are millions of women out there in bad or even abusive marriages who continually talk of leaving one day, but never do. I knew they were right. Most of the time it's probably due to a lack of resources to help them, financially or emotionally. I felt that with the combination of my devoted, unquestionable love for her and my financial resources that I could alleviate all of her fears and help drive her to the Promised Land where we could live happily ever after."

For the next five years, Gus and Lisa continued their love affair. Gus never pressured her to leave her husband, neither did he foist any expectations or time table upon her. He and Lisa would giddily talk about all the things they would do one day when they could finally be together.

She also conveyed her misgivings and trepidations of leaving her husband. She told Gus that she felt certain that her husband would take the house in a divorce. "Where will I live?" she would ask Gus. Remarkably, Gus bought her a condo in the part of town that Lisa had always dreamed of living. Lisa was overwhelmed by this gesture, but quickly asserted that her husband would get all of the furniture, and she didn't have the money to furnish her new lovely place. So Gus financed a whirlwind of furniture shopping, buying her a house worth of furniture fit for a hopeful bride. Whatever the concern, whatever the fear or obstacle was, Gus and his bazooka would blow through it, eliminating her anxieties one by one. Finally, eight years into their relationship, five years after Gus left his wife, Lisa agreed to see an attorney, for which, yes, Gus eagerly footed the bill.

Of course we all know how this story ends and if you, the reader, would like to turn the page to the next chapter, by all means go ahead. I wish I could.

A few weeks after seeing the attorney, Lisa told Gus that she couldn't go through with the divorce. After she told her husband about seeing an attorney, she said her husband immediately accepted a transfer to the west coast, a transfer that his boss had been offering him for some time. "He says a change of scenery will do us good," she told Gus. "He assures me things will be different this time. My family needs me Gus. I can't let them down."

Gus bowed his head with a heavy heart. It wasn't enough that he was losing his best friend and love of his life. He realized at that moment that his immense love matched with all the money in the world would never get Lisa past her insecurities and fears. She left him, promising to write once they were settled down and let him know where they would be residing.

Gus drove by her street the afternoon that she was set to move. He parked the car down the street and watched the moving truck as it pulled out of the driveway. Lisa was leaving him, leaving him with a condo full of furniture and a broken heart.

Gus never did get that letter. "That's what stings the most," admitted Gus. "I was so stupid, stupid for waiting patiently for eight years for something that I should have known was never going to happen. Deep inside, she probably knew in her gut she'd never leave. Our loving commitment to be together one day was as much a façade as her marriage. I need to stop now and get a martini."

I asked Gus a couple more questions but he stopped me. "You know the whole story. I've omitted almost nothing except for the tears I shed for a long time."

Gus is seventy years old now. He's still single. One can understand his reluctance to get involved in another relationship considering his history. His social life is pretty much centered around the local senior center these days. "I don't know why I keep going back there, everyone is so old," he laughs.

He says he is OK now and at peace, although he still hates to open the mailbox during those periods surrounding his birthday or Christmas. I asked him if there's anything besides martinis that helps get him through those times he begins to think about her.

He then told me for many years he has secretly loved a sonnet by Edna St. Vincent Mallay. He particularly likes the lines:

> I stand here like a lonely tree
> I know not where the birds have gone nor why,
> I only see the branches more empty than before.
> I cannot say what loves have come and gone
> I only know that summer once sang in me.

For Gus's sake, I hope that winter ends soon and that spring is around the corner.

The story of Gus is one that still gets to me to this day. The magnitude of his love for Lisa is exemplified in the never-ending endeavors he took to unite them together. Unfortunately, Gus mistakenly thought that he could make Lisa leave her husband if he only did enough things for her. The truth is that in the end, Lisa was going to do what Lisa was going to do, regardless of what he was willing to do for her. That, of course, is the primary lesson of Gus's story. But the secondary message was that Gus's unremitting optimism throughout their eight year relationship, although romantically admirable, only garnered him a broken heart which ails him to this day. Gus's glossy eyed optimism hindered his ability to recognize a simple truth, that the longer someone repeatedly talks about their Someday without doing anything, the more certain that they will do nothing in the end.

Having an optimistic attitude about life in general is a good thing, but blind optimism can guide us into dangerous waters. Life is all about balance, and in the next chapter, we will take a closer look at what optimism really is.

Optimistic Pessimism

"Everybody dies ... The thing is, to have a life before we die."

- John Irving, The World According to Garp

During the immediate aftermath of the housing bubble that began in 2006/07, I met several people who were attempting to sell their house. I say attempting because there was a seemingly limitless supply of homes supplemented by too few buyers and it was obvious they were pricing their homes far beyond the real market value. Occasionally I would suggest to one of those sellers that they might want to lower the price to which they would say something like, "I don't need your negative energy. I know this house is going to sell," or "Maybe you aren't optimistic about my house selling, but I am."

Of course I wasn't trying to be negative or positive, I was simply offering advice based on the reality of the situation. Reality is neither optimistic nor pessimistic, it simply is what it is. In the meantime, nine months would pass by with not even a nibble on their house. At that point they would finally reduce the price. Unfortunately, they would reduce it to the price they should have opened with in the first place and the market now was even worse, which meant that their new asking price was much too high yet again. This is a phenomenon real estate agents refer to as "chasing the market." According to real estate sites such as Trulia.com and real estate giants such as Remax, the data is very clear that sellers who chase the market end up far worse off than people who get a little ahead of a failing real estate market and just get out. The fact is, all the optimism in the world isn't going to bring a sucker who is willing to overpay for a house that the market clearly says is going downhill even further.

Just prior to the Great Recession, I began sensing the storm clouds on the horizon. I didn't know what exactly was coming, nor how bad it would be. I had a strong premonition that something was about to change and it didn't seem promising. I began taking precautionary steps to prepare my family for the storm. I sold our boat, one of our cars and took on a third job as well. People accused me of being Mr. Doom and Gloom back then. They said I was a pessimistic person.

Yes, I was pessimistic about the macro world at that time, which turned out to be a correct intuition. In fact, if anything, I wasn't gloomy enough. However, at the same time, I was very optimistic about myself and my family's ability to weather the turbulent times ahead. Thanks to the large ticket items we sold and my additional job, we had reinforced our cash reserves and paid off some of our debt. Like an army preparing for an impending attack from a stronger force, I had refortified my position substantially and now had the high ground. Was I scared? Of course, but I was optimistic now because I knew the reality of the situation and had prepared for it. In summary, the impending reality I felt coming, made me pessimistic enough to take the necessary steps to now be optimistic.

In the pop culture psychology world of today, people often equate optimism as some magical force such as in the movie Star Wars. People think that with a strong dose of optimism and a light saber, they can defeat all of the Darth Vaders of the world. Yes, Luke Skywalker was able to do so, and yes he had the force with him. He also had years of intensive training as a Jedi Knight. In order for a Jedi candidate to obtain the title of Jedi Knight they had to overcome a series of presubscribed tests that measured their skill set and courage. This was culminated by the accomplishment of something of grandeur and significance such as when Obi-Wan kills the Sith Lord in battle. In the end, it was this designed process that probably had more to do with his ability to handle Lord Vader than anything else.

Too often we use optimism as an excuse to put off our Someday. How many times do you hear a woman with a domineering callous husband say that she'll be able to "change him" over time, rather than deal with the situation at hand and leave him? Yes, it's optimistic to think that he might change one magical day. It's also easier because it avoids the conflict of leaving him. How many of us in a dead-end job keep telling ourselves that things will get better, rather than finding a new work environment which will allow them to flourish? That takes work however. It requires one to deal with change, and change is scary. It's easier to stay in that cubicle and be "optimistic" about tomorrow.

Blind optimism is easy. Taking the required steps to achieve your Someday is much more difficult, which is why so many of us cling to optimism.

The best example I can think of in how to look at optimism is college football. Although I never went to the University of Georgia, I am a fan of their football team. Like many of the top college football programs in the country, the Georgia Bulldogs play a couple of cream puffs every year. They do this to give the team a couple of easy games so they can focus on the big rivalry game that comes the following week. These easy games are guaranteed victories the vast majority of the time so they help inflate the number of wins for the season. The athletic director of the smaller schools agree to these games because they can make more money off a single game with a school like UGA than they can make the entire season. This is because a popular Division I school like UGA with a history of winning can pull nearly a hundred thousand fans into the stadium on a given Saturday, while a typical smaller school can only attract twenty thousand fans at best.

These are smaller schools, usually in a lesser division.

These smaller schools don't have the resources to match a large school like the University of Georgia in football with its history of football excellence. Their first string players don't match up against those of UGA in size, speed or talent. The disparity when comparing the second string of each team is even more lopsided. These games tend to be blowouts, especially in the third and fourth quarters as Georgia's roster depth begins to take over the game.

These games tend to end up with Georgia winning with something like 48 to 10. It would be an even bigger whipping if it weren't for the fact that the coach of Georgia usually pulls out the starters in the fourth quarter and begins calling a pretty conservative game plan so as not to embarrass the other team.

So what does the coach of the visiting small school tell his team in the locker room just before the game? Surely he doesn't tell them that they are going to absolutely win the game. That would be unrealistic.

He probably tells them how the game today is a lesson about overcoming adversity and great odds. That they are going to go out there and play the game of their life on a stage larger than life. He probably tells them that today they get to see, as individuals, how they match up against the very best. That he wants them to play a mistake free game and a game they can look back on and be proud of. That if they can play a competitive game against a team like the one they are about to confront on the field, that they can beat anyone on their schedule the rest of the year.

In other words, he is optimistic, not about getting an absolute victory, but about how they deal with the challenges at hand. Because even if they don't win, they can still tell their grandchildren years from now that they played football once in front of a crowd of over a hundred thousand. They and their teammates can boast how they stopped a superior team on a fourth down goal line stand. The quarterback can always remember how he didn't throw a single interception despite playing against an elite secondary.

In other words, the team may leave that grand stadium that day without a win, but some can leave with personal victories, because it is only at a personal level that we can control things. And those team members who are optimistic about their own personal abilities are the ones most likely to achieve greatness that day. Just as Gus's actions at a personal level couldn't change the relationship between Lisa and her domineering husband, a division two school cannot will itself a victory over an elite division one school.

But at a micro level, we can accomplish whatever we want, even when things look their darkest at the macro level.

And sometimes, when each member of that small division two team is attaining levels of personal greatness, and the team plays a perfect game, on a day when the elite division one school thought they could just phone it in, sometimes, or should we say, Somedays, the lesser team pulls out a victory. It's those rare victories that give us hope, hope that if we all work towards achieving greatness at a personal level, that we can change the world collectively.

A Long Heritage of Optimism

"The American, by nature, is optimistic. He is experimental, an inventor and a builder who builds best when called upon to build greatly."

- John F. Kennedy

While blind optimism doesn't necessarily do us any good, a healthy dose of optimism is essential to keep us marching towards our Someday. In fact America is one of the most optimistic nations on earth. It seems to be a part of our very nature. Why is it that we as Americans are so inheritably optimistic is a subject of debate but a great explanation as to why comes from historian, Frederick Jackson Turner, who in 1893, published his hypothesis entitled the "Frontier Theory."

Turner believed that many of the characteristics associated with the American people were traceable to their experience during the three centuries our nation spent settling the continent. The constant willingness of Americans during this 300 year period to head to the next frontier and "begin a new life" was fueled by heavy doses of optimism, inventiveness and a willingness to accept innovation. Their tendency to view the world through rose-colored glasses gave them the will and alacrity to make repeated trips out west despite the hardships and challenges that were constantly foisted on them. They were dreamers. For them, the frontier was a horizon of hope. The frontier represented a second chance, to erase the mistakes of their past and start fresh with a clean slate and a new attitude. It was an opportunity to take the wisdom from the lessons they had learned from their past and apply it in a new environment in order to attain their dreams and aspirations of a better life.

Let's say that you lived in Boston at around the turn of the 19th century and life wasn't that great for you. You were short on opportunities and even shorter on cash. You couldn't seem to find your rightful place in such a big established city. You felt like you needed someplace that wasn't established as of yet, a place that you could get in at the very beginning and build something. With its virgin land that remained unscarred from man, the Ohio Territories seemed like the perfect place to do just that.

So you sold what belongings you deemed unessential for your pilgrimage, hitched your wagon and slowly trekked westward. You arrived in the Ohio Territories and made a new start for yourself. With the wisdom generated from your prior experiences, you made more judicious decisions and approached things a little differently the second go-around. Still, despite your best efforts, life still wasn't what you imagined it to be.

And then you heard the news, there's Gold in them hills, in the hills of California. The Gold Rush was on and you knew that this was your one opportunity to cash in on this while the door was still open and the iron was hot. You imagined yourself striking it rich and then cashing it out so that you could live it up and relax for the rest of your life in comfort and style. Again, you packed up, loaded the cart and led the family westward once more in search of fortune that this time around you were sure would be yours.

You arrived in California and soon discovered that panning for gold was a lot of back breaking work that required a great deal of skill, energy and a large dose of luck. You did manage to find a few nuggets during that time but the mother lode you romanticized about discovering continually eluded you.

And then you heard that they were offering two million acres of cheap land in Oklahoma to whoever wanted to lay claim to it. You knew this could be your last chance to be the established land owner you always envisioned as the vast majority of the country had been settled by now. Yet again, you rushed your family, eastward this time, to the Promised Land where you would stake out a few acres of heaven for you and your family. Maybe you stayed in Oklahoma for the remainder of your life, maybe you didn't.

Thus a habitual pattern was established in America that continues to this day. Look at the fluidness of our country as people who grew up in Ohio head to Georgia, while people in Georgia head to Washington

State and people in Washington State head to North Dakota. This is who we are as Americans. We are a nation of dreamers and builders. We are a nation of people who believe that tomorrow will be a better day simply because we dream it.

Thanks to those brave settlers and frontiersmen, we as Americans continue their heritage of hope and optimism, asserting that life in the future will definitely be better Someday when I move to . . .

Stop Trying to Make Everyone Happy

"I have learned that pleasing everyone is impossible, but pissing everyone off is a piece of cake!"

- An Anonymous Facebook Posting

You can't make everyone happy!

That is a fact. It is an unattainable fallacy. For starters, you can't know what makes everyone happy, only what you think makes them happy. Everyone has different motivations, values, perspectives, temperaments and so on. Since you can't possibly know what makes each individual happy, there is no way to ensure that everyone is.

Think about all of your friends, relatives and co-workers. You couldn't get this assortment of people to agree on what single flavor of ice cream to buy. How are you going to make everyone happy with an upcoming decision you have to make?

Face it, occasionally you are going to upset people around you and, OMG – they will be unhappy sometimes.

Colin Powell said it best:

> "Pissing people off is both inevitable and necessary. This doesn't mean that the goal is pissing people off. Pissing people off doesn't mean you're doing the right things, but doing the right things will almost inevitably piss people off."

He goes on to say:

> "Trying to get everyone to like you is a sign of mediocrity: you'll avoid the tough decisions, you'll avoid confronting the people who need to be confronted, and you'll avoid offering differential rewards based on differential performance because some people might get upset.

> "Ironically, by procrastinating on the difficult choices, by trying not to get anyone mad, and by treating everyone equally and 'nicely' regardless of their contributions, you'll simply ensure that the only people you'll wind up angering are the most creative and productive people in the organization."

First off, there isn't enough time in the day, nor do you have the energy to make everyone happy. Making so many people happy is exhausting. It zaps you of all of your energy, energy that then can't be directed to the people who mean the most in your life. When you are trying to make everyone happy, you don't have time for much else. Most people can't even make themselves happy, yet they expect to be able to achieve nirvana for everyone around them.

People who attempt to make everyone happy are trying to be jugglers. You can easily learn to juggle tennis balls, apples or bowling pins. It's tough to juggle the multiple needs of people.

Secondly, when someone says, "I just want to make everyone happy," what they are really saying is that they are going to treat everyone the same. The person who lives two-thousand miles away is given equal treatment as the person who lives close by. Making the mail clerk happy is equally as important as the person who signs your paycheck. The person who is always there for you whenever you need them, is allotted the same treatment as the person who only contacts you when they need something.

The fact is, you have to prioritize people in your life. People expect it. The business owner who took a chance by hiring you even though you lacked some experience expects to be treated with greater service and respect. The people who are always there for you and love you emphatically expect you to make them a priority in their lives above all others. The person who is in love with you expects to be allotted more priority than just an acquaintance.

This is just a fact of life.

And what happens when you don't prioritize the people who expect you to? At some point they stop prioritizing you as well. Relationships work like a two-way street like that. People who make you feel special, who go out of their way for you and who always come through for you, expect to be treated likewise.

Make a list right now of the five or six most important people in your life. These are the people who are the most vested within your life. Treat all of your kids as one person collectively. These people should receive priority above all others. They are the ones you worry about when making a decision. Hopefully you put your name down as one of the five because you are the most important person of all. If not, remove someone from the list and insert your name. Put it at the top of the list as well.

And what about people who aren't on the list? Don't integrate their needs into a decision making process when it comes to your happiness. For instance, if you keep putting off moving to the beach because you love your neighbors and you know they would hate to see you move away from the neighborhood, forget about them. Do you really think they are going to forego an opportunity to move to the beach because of you?

A lady I know is married to an atrocious jerk that makes her life miserable.

"Why don't you leave him?" everyone asks her.

"I can't do that," she says. "What would my mom and my Aunt Jillian think? It would kill them. What would they tell their neighbors when they asked about me?"

Meanwhile mom and Aunt Jillian live over two-thousand miles away. They get together with her for Christmas every year, maybe every other summer. Meanwhile, she is the one who has to live with her abusing nemeses every day of her life so as not to upset mom and Aunt Julian.

But what about my kids you may ask? Until they leave my house, I should focus on their happiness, shouldn't I?

Yes, up to a point, a parent needs to put the needs of their kids above theirs. However, doesn't a happy mommy or daddy make a better parent than a miserable one? Don't you think your kids want to see you enjoying life as well? Of course they do. As parents, we all need to focus on our own health and happiness to ensure that we are able to perform our parenting duties.

As parents, we lead by example as well. Don't you want to demonstrate to your kids that their own happiness is most important, rather than have them go through life trying to please everyone around them, like you are, which you have found doesn't work so well?

Many people put off their Someday because they are so busy trying to make everyone happy. They never speak their mind or express their opinion on matters because they are afraid they might offend someone. They never take a risk or do something crazy because it might invite gossip amongst members of their social circle who may look down at such behavior. They never make time to finish that degree they never started or completed or take a cooking class because the kids or spouse might be disturbed about their absence for a few hours every week.

But guess what? Have you ever noticed that those same people who you are so afraid to upset or have their feathers ruffled don't' seem to have any trouble going with decisions that make you unhappy? It's not that they aren't interested in your happiness, it's just that they are putting the needs of themselves first. And you should put your own needs first as well when it comes to anyone outside of those five or six critically important people you put on your list.

Trying to make everyone happy around you usually produces the opposite effect in that no one is happy, especially you. This is one of the ironies in trying to please everyone. It makes you miserable because you always find yourself sacrificing your needs and relinquishing your dreams for someone's happiness, who probably wouldn't do the same for you. Remember, when Father Time pulls into your driveway in his sports car, it's the joyous moments that you experienced throughout your life - not the moments of others – are those that will truly matter.

You Really Don't Need All of that Stuff

*"Well, I'm running down the road tryin' to loosen my
load
I've got seven women on my mind,
Four that wanna own me, Two that wanna stone me,
One says she's a friend of mine
Take It easy, take it easy
Don't let the sound of your own wheels drive you crazy
Lighten up while you still can, don't even try to
understand
Just find a place to make your stand, and take it easy"*

- The Eagles

One of my favorite movies is "Up in the Air" starring George Clooney. Clooney plays a corporate executive named Ryan Bingam, who constantly travels the country doing what he does best, firing people in a personable way that presumably lessens the pain of being terminated. In addition to his regular job, Bingam is trying to make it as a seminar speaker promoting his lifestyle of mobility and minimalism. Standing at a lectern, he delivers a thought-provoking speech in which he asks the question: What is in your backpack? Bingam addresses the audience:

"How much does your life weigh? Imagine for a second that you're carrying a backpack. I want

you to feel the straps on your shoulders. Feel 'em? Now I want you to pack it with all the stuff that you have in your life. You start with the little things. The things on shelves and in drawers, the knick-knacks, the collectibles. Feel the weight as that adds up. Then you start adding larger stuff, clothes, table-top appliances, lamps, linens, your TV. The backpack should be getting pretty heavy now. And you go bigger. Your couch, bed, your kitchen table. Stuff it all in there. Your car, get it in there. Your home, whether it's a studio apartment or a two bedroom house. I want you to stuff it all into that backpack. Now try to walk. It's kind of hard, isn't it? This is what we do to ourselves on a daily basis. We weigh ourselves down until we can't even move. And make no mistake, moving is living. Now, I'm gonna set that backpack on fire. What do you want to take out of it? What do you want to take out of it? Photos? Photos are for people who can't remember. Drink some ginkgo and let the photos burn. In fact, let everything burn and imagine waking up tomorrow with nothing. It's kind of exhilarating, isn't it?"

Let's face it. We Americans own a lot of stuff. More stuff than we know what to do with. We have stuff we use every day, stuff we need, stuff we think we need, stuff we think we may need one day, and stuff that we know we don't need at all, but we keep it anyway. We keep so much stuff that one in ten Americans rents a public storage unit. Depending on whom you ask, there are enough public storage units in this country to allot every man, woman and child seven square feet of storage. And while we have been carting stuff to our nearby public storage facility, our closets and homes have concurrently gotten larger.

We have such a difficult time parting with our stuff that the impact of a weak economy has had a negligible impact of only 2 or 3 percent on the public storage industry. Derek Naylor, president of the consulting group, Storage Marketing Solutions, explains why: "Once they're in, nobody likes to spend all day moving their stuff out of storage. As long as they can afford it, and feel psychologically that they can afford it, they'll leave that stuff in there forever."

And why are they leaving that stuff in storage units forever? Probably for the same reason that they leave all that stuff down in the basement: because everyone in the house hates having to rearrange so much stuff! They leave that stuff there because they might need it, or want it, one day.

Yes, they *might*.

There's a lot of stuff I *might* need one day. I *might* need a litter box if I own a cat one day. I *might* need a set of golf clubs if I ever learn to play golf. I *might* need a fire iron if I ever own a house with a fireplace. I *might* need to own a number of things, and if I ever do . . . . I can buy them at a good price at a nearby store.

In the book, "Minimalism, Live a Meaningful Life," the authors point out how much time, energy and money we spend on keeping all that stuff. Let's face it; everyone hates that daunting task of organizing the endless amount of stuff in the basement when mom obsesses with "spring cleaning" every year. Now, start adding up how much all of that extra storage space in your house actually costs you, including the cost of heating and cooling those areas. Next, add up how much you are doling out every month for that public storage unit while your stuff isn't even accessible to you unless you get in a car and drive to it.

Stuff drags us down, even the stuff we think we need. The bizarre irony of the housing bubble induced recession is that millions of Americans spent hundreds of thousands of dollars on their "dream home." Then, the recession came, and many of them lost their jobs. Some of them were offered jobs on the other side of town, or in another state, but they couldn't take those jobs because they couldn't sell the "dream house" that made them happy.

And then, their "dream house" turned into a nightmare.

So many people were just plain stuck. They were stuck in a house they couldn't sell, leaving them in a hopeless financial situation. What a difference a few years makes. Just think how many people wished they had never purchased that "dream house." Those granite counter tops that were so important a few years earlier now deemed them as mobile as a granite mine, preventing them from adapting to the economic challenges they faced.

Think about how mobile the world is today. We can pull our cellphones out of our pockets and talk to anyone in the country. We can get on our laptops and browse the Internet or Skype with anyone in the world. We can hop in the car and travel cross-country, or get on a jet plane and travel to the other side of the globe, all within hours. We live in a world of seamless mobility.

And yet, we tie ourselves down by owning lots of stuff that stifles our freedom to move.. Companies today have learned that in order to thrive in today's economy, they must be lean and nimble enough to instantly adjust to evolving situations on a continual basis. Companies have shed themselves of overhead and discarded unnecessary assets in the name of economic survival. Yet, we as individuals continue to saddle ourselves with more and more stuff that suffocates us.

If things made us happy, then children today would be far happier than children of past generations were. Kids today have far more possessions than their predecessors did, but they clearly aren't any happier. Parents race around every holiday and birthday trying to obtain the latest gadget or toy for their child, even though his or her closet is already overrun with last year's "must-have" toys and gadgets. A computer game is a great way for a child to kill time, but what really makes children happy is interacting with other kids, or with their parents. Think about the baby who prefers playing with the wrapping paper that encased the present they just opened to playing with the present itself. Children demonstrate that it's the simple things in life that truly make us the happiest. Of course, you may not have time to observe your children to that degree because you are working so hard to pay for all of that stuff.

In a book entitled, "How Much is Enough," authored by University of Warwick Professor Emeritus, Robert Skidelsky, he poses the age old question: "Does money make you happy?" Skidelsky alludes to a set of "basic goods" that compose a happy life including: health, education, leisure, friendship and harmony with nature. The author states that happiness is a state of mind, a state of mind attained by people of all income levels.

So how much does your backpack weigh? How much is it dragging you down and tiring you out before you ever get any sort of momentum toward achieving your Someday? Think about the money and the energy you could redirect towards the attainment of your Someday if it wasn't being consumed by all of that stuff you haven't used in five years.

When it comes right down to it, all of that stuff is nothing more than that, just stuff. On the other hand, your Someday is what dreams are made of. You probably can't even remember what you received for your birthday last year, but you can recite what your

Someday is, because that is what's most important. Stop being obsessed with stuff and empty your backpack! Realize that those material things you covet cost you more than just the price tag at the time of purchase. Those things tie you down, demanding and diverting your resources from other things like your dreams. March ahead towards your Someday!

It's Pronounced Nnnnnnnnnooooooooooo

"The art of leadership is saying no, not yes. It is very easy to say yes."

- Tony Blair

When it comes to people, it's impossible to keep some things under wrap. For instance, it doesn't take long for the word to spread that "there's gold in them hills," as rumors of the latest gold discovery initiate a flood of prospectors dreaming of striking it rich. It doesn't take long for word to spread that the new I-Phone comes out next Friday, resulting in people lining up in front of the store days beforehand to ensure that they are the first one on the block to own the newest prize. And finally, word spreads very fast within a company, church or neighborhood that there's a new guy or gal who doesn't know how to say No. Once that bit of news gets out, everyone begins lining up to ask him or her to do their bidding for them. People love folks who can't say No.

There are many clichés about people who can't say No. There's the old adage that 20% of the people in a group do 80% of the work. It's because many of the people that make up that 20% can't say No. It's also easy to pass the buck to people who can't say No.

Elton John wrote the lyric: "Sorry seems to be the hardest word" in one of his famous songs. He was wrong. "No" is the hardest word. And people love folks who can't say No. Think about it. It's easy being the parent who always says Yes. Saying Yes to your kids whenever they ask you for candy in the grocery checkout lane is easy. It's easy to say Yes to that new video the kids want so that they will stay quiet for a few hours. Being a politician who always says Yes to every government giveaway program is easy because people vote for the politician who always says Yes. It's easy to say Yes to everyone who asks you to do them a favor because it avoids the conflict of having to say No to a friend, co-worker or relative. When it isn't expected, or is rarely used, the word No can be a controversial word, and the word No doesn't make people very happy.

Saying Yes, is easy, but as is typical in life, the easy way isn't necessarily the best way. It usually results in consequences down the road. Constantly saying Yes to your kids every time they beg for candy in the grocery checkout lane keeps them quiet in the short term, but can negatively impact their dental health and weight in the long term. Constantly doling out new government programs is easy to do to garner votes in the short term, but in the long term, someone has to pay for those programs, which always impacts the economy in some unforeseen manner.

And, constantly saying Yes to everyone at your church,

your school PTA, place of employment, not to mention your neighbors and relatives, might be easy too. Don't kid yourself though, there are long term consequences for playing the perpetual errand boy or girl.

The fact is that you only have so much time and energy each and every day. If you are always expending your limited resources on others, you can't utilize them for the things that are important to you. How can you see the fruition of your Someday when you are constantly filling your time serving everyone else? And guess what, one of the reasons that some people constantly ask for your help is to free up their time so they can do the things that they want to do!

This isn't to say you shouldn't help your friends and colleagues, far from it. Life isn't only about selfishly serving ourselves. It's about helping others too. When you do a good deed for someone, it makes you feel good knowing that you are aiding your fellow man. When you and your neighbors pull your efforts together and help each other, life is easier for everyone. Occasionally, your neighbor needs you to watch his or her dog when they go off on a long weekend. You may need them to pick your son up from football practice because you are running late at work. When it comes to everyday life, it does take a village.

But, if you look at people who can't say No, you usually see a very one-sided arrangement. Just like children fail to appreciate a gift when they constantly get whatever they want, no one appreciates the person who never says No. Just as the spoiled child takes new toys for granted, people take Yes for granted when it is assumed. Consequently, it's easy for those people who never say No to begin feeling taken for granted, which can lead to resentment and frustration. The problem is that by now, the inertia that prevents the utterance of the word No is so great, that it is difficult to overcome.

One day, I was talking to an elementary school cafeteria manager at the school my daughter attends. Although it was the responsibility of the cafeteria staff to prepare the snack for the after school program each day, it wasn't their job to serve the snack to the children. However, the teacher in charge of the after school program would ask this cafeteria manager to deliver the snack to the kids every single day, a task that added an extra 45 minutes to her workday. As a result, she left 45 minutes later every day. What's more, she was never compensated for these additional 45 minutes of work because after all, it wasn't a part of her job description. It also took her away from her responsibility as a mother as she had a special-needs child who required much more attention than the average child. Many days she needed to take him to see a doctor, speech therapist or some other specialist after school, forcing her to rush through the day in order to try and gain as much of the 45 minutes back as possible.

So each and every day, the manager found herself in the assumed role of dispersing the after school program snack. She never received recognition for helping out every day. Finally, months later, she informed the teacher that she just couldn't continue to assist day in and day out as she was getting home late nearly every day.

"What about teamwork?" sniped the teacher. "Don't you believe in teamwork?"

The cafeteria manager didn't want to be accused of not being a team player and immediately backed down, resuming her thankless extracurricular duties. A couple days later, someone suggested to her that she remind the after school teacher that teamwork involves two players. Since she was running late every day due to distributing the after school snack, why not ask the teacher to reciprocate by coming down to the cafeteria during her break every day so that the cafeteria manager could leave on time That way, it would be a true team effort.

After the cafeteria manager approached her with this proposition, the teacher never asked for her help again. It seems that the definition of "team effort" is different with some people.

Be willing to help your neighbors when they are in need, but don't be afraid to say No to those routine, repetitive requests full of assumption and void of appreciation. Don't feel guilty because you have things to do for yourself, such as working towards the culmination of your Someday!

The fact is that saying No sometimes will mean that

when someone asks you later in life if you ever did write that book, or get to Paris, or start that business, you can say:

YES!

Don't Forget the Magic of Life

"I do not exist to impress the world. I exist to live my life in a way that will make me happy. "

- Richard Bach

During the 90's, I produced and released a series of CD's featuring my instrumental compositions. Music had been a major part of my life ever since my mother signed me up for piano lessons when I was six years old. I quickly discovered that I had a gift for music and that my hands felt at home on the keys. It soon became obvious that I had a talent and that I had the motivation to cultivate it into something great.

I spent countless hours growing up playing scales, arpeggios, Bach preludes and sonatinas by Clemente. In high school, I discovered rock and roll. After seeing Billy Joel live in concert with my dad on a transformational night, I purchased a Rhodes electronic piano in lieu of the Yamaha MX 175 dirt bike I had been saving my money to buy. As I had a troublesome stuttering problem throughout my childhood, I found the piano to be the perfect outlet to audibly express those thoughts that I was too timid to express verbally. I would sit in our family basement for hours at a time, talking with my Rhodes piano about the problems I encountered earlier that day, and about the girl I had my eye on but was too nervous to approach.

In high school, I quickly rose up through the ranks of garage bands throughout my teenage years, until I was able to hand pick the musicians with whom I desired to make music. As I was deciding where to attend college after graduation, I enrolled in one of the top music schools in the country in order to find out how good I really was at playing the piano. Consequently, I became a minnow in a sea of musical masters all around me. It was the best thing I could have done. Always put yourself in an environment in which you aren't at the top of the pyramid, as that only leads to indolence. Its competition that makes you better, and life is about constantly making improving yourself. You either grow, or you fade away, it is the law of evolution.

I took a stab at a professional music career after graduating college, but got tired of "making peanuts" in a decade when the classic movie character, Gordon Gecko, from the movie, Wall Street, was preaching that "greed is good." I was making less than twenty grand a year and working three jobs. I wanted to make my first million dollars and stake my claim in the world with a stack of money, rather than a stack of something I created. So, I decided to trade in my piano chops for suit pants and suspenders and pursue my fortune.

But, a recession-induced downsizing by my employer a few years later clipped my dreams of a "Wall Street fortune" before I could achieve any real momentum. While managing a job search that was going nowhere, I returned to my music as a refuge and a stressor release. Having learned how to market myself, I had a conception now of how to promote my music to the public. Having matured myself since my first attempt at stardom, my music had a far more developed sound. This combination allowed me to garner some energy and enthusiasm for my music.

I recorded, and produced, my first album. It was a true labor of love. There was a story behind each and every track I recorded. Each piece told a short narrative, and the compilation itself told a story of my life, a life with which I hoped that others could connect. Still unemployed, I had a minimal budget, and my initial production was released in cassette form only.

I now had a couple boxes of cassettes that I needed to distribute. I booked a performance at a local Unity Church, whose congregation was known to appreciate soothing, melodic instrumental music. After packing up all of my keyboards and synthesizers for the gig, I haphazardly threw a couple dozen of my cassettes into my duffle bag, thinking that it would be more than enough in my attempt to sell my music afterwards.

At the conclusion of my performance, I hustled out into the lobby to man my table, where I hoped to sell a few of my cassettes. They sold out in a matter of minutes. I could have sold twice as many that day. I even took a few orders for which people wrote me a check on the promise I would mail them one of my cassettes. I was elated and on top of the world. People were purchasing my music. My music had been substantiated by complete strangers. They appreciated my sound enough to part with their hard earned money to bring my music into their home. I was touched and honored.

Later that day I was mowing my front lawn. That's how life is you know, one minute you are a music maharishi and the next minute you are doing something as normal and mundane as yard work. As I maneuvered the lawn mower in straight lines back and forth on that hot summer day, my mind began to daydream as I tried to envision what the purchasers of my cassettes were doing at that moment. I wondered if they were listening to my music as I mowed, marveling at the very idea that they could be enjoying a glass of wine in their living room as they listened to my music over their high-end sound system. Maybe they were enjoying a Sunday drive, listening to my music as they drove to the mountains to escape the heat of a hot summer day in Georgia. Maybe they were sharing my music with friends and family who would be calling me later in the week to obtain their own personal copy. I had received compliments about my music for much of my life, but on that day, the wallets and purses of 24 strangers validated the quality of my music. It was truly a magical day.

I began to contemplate that this could be the start of a wave that I could ride for years to come and hire someone to mow my lawn at my future chateau.

Unfortunately, I soon became impervious to the magical appreciation of people purchasing my music. Within a matter of years, it was no longer about the music. It was simply about the number of units sold. As soon I as I would get in the car with my wife, or with whomever I had hired to manage my booth and sell my music during and after my performances, I would ask how many units we had sold.

"We sold 80 units," they would answer, and I would verbally display my displeasure at the figure. "We should have sold a hundred for a show like this," I would answer in a very unappreciative manner. No matter how many we sold it was never enough. I could no longer focus on the eighty people who had bought my music and were playing it in their personal world. It was now simply about the lowest common denominator in life. It became all about the money.

In 1976, Peter Frampton came out with his historic album, "Frampton Comes Alive," historic because it sold more than ten million copies and held the title of best-selling live album of all time for twenty years. In a documentary about rock and roll, Frampton confesses that after the popularity of that album, he approached music from the perspective of, "What can I write that 'they' will want to hear?" He would forever measure his music by units sold, not by the message it conveyed, or the magical process that created it. As a result, he never came close to matching the fame and popularity he attained with that iconic album. His career floundered. People don't want to hear music that you think they want to hear, they want to hear music that comes from the heart. That's where the magic is.

To the common man, the creative process of making music is magical, as the musician or composer takes an inspiration and transcribes it into audible harmonious melody, entrenching itself within us. Music is the ideal medium with which to record life because life and love are both magical. Many of us use songs to conjure up our memories of yesteryear. Our favorite song has the ability to carry us back to a particular time and place. Music reminds us of the magic of life, which is why music has such meaning to us.

It's when we forget the magic of life that we begin to sell ourselves short. It's when we forget about how astonishing life can be that we settle for the dead end job. It's when we forget how enchanting life can be that we forget about what dreams are made of. It's when we forget how truly breathtaking it actually is that we are on this planet that life becomes mundane. It's when we take life for granted that we forget how to appreciate love. When you forget the magic of life, you end up just mowing the grass without enjoying the daydream that allows you to escape the monotony of it all.

British poet, Arthur O'Shaughnessy said, "We are the music makers, and we are the dreamers of dreams." You don't have to play a major scale on the piano to make music. You don't have to play a I-V-I power chord progression on the guitar. Making music is about living life to its fullest and savoring every day.

We are all composers, painters and poets. Life itself is our blank canvas and our tablet of manuscript paper. Truly living life means never forgetting the magic of it.

When it comes to music; however, Bob Dylan said it best: "Play it fuckin loud!"

In other words, play your life loudly, for it is a magnanimous melody that is worthy of being heard. So go play it loudly, and let the world know who you are.

Someday is a Great Day

"This is really a dream come true. To be the starting quarterback in the super bowl is probably the highlight of my life."

- Tom Brady

I am an avid football fan, and one of my favorite legendary stories is that of the Los Angeles Rams defensive end, Jack Youngblood. In 1979, he broke his fibula in a Divisional playoff game against the Dallas Cowboys. A broken leg, such as this, would constitute a season ending injury to most any football player, but not in the case of Jack Youngblood, Jack merely exited to the sidelines and demanded that the trainers tape up his leg. He then proceeded to complete the game, contributing to the upset victory over the Cowboys that day. After the game, he wrapped his leg in a plastic cast. Through the combination of a freakish pain threshold and an iron will to proceed towards his dream of playing in the Super Bowl, Youngblood suited up and played a week later in the NFC Championship Game, where he helped to defeat the Tampa Bay Buccaneers in a shutout. He played again the following week in a Super Bowl Matchup against the Pittsburgh Steelers, which the Rams unfortunately lost 31-19.

When asked how he was able to withstand the seemingly unbearable pain on the field, Jack simply replied, "This was my chance to go to the Super Bowl. Nothing was going to stop me."

Jack saw his Someday come to fruition, and the throbbing pain of his leg wasn't going to dull the greatness of it.

Someday is a great day!

There are going to be some disappointing moments now and then in the quest towards your Someday. There will be setbacks and days where it seems as if you're moving two steps back, for every step you take forward. There are going to be days when you will want to throw your hands up in the air in abandonment of your dream. And on those days, focus on how great your Someday is going to be. Remember Jack Youngblood, who played three football games with a broken leg!

Though the tale of Jack's amazing triumph over pain in his journey towards the Super Bowl is a heroic story, his journey to that Someday began during the preseason. Jack and his teammates collectively worked out, honed their skills, digested the playbook and practiced their implementations of key plays and game scenarios. It was a long journey, full of hard work, and it was worth every bead of sweat and every sore muscle ache.

Former NFL head coach of the Indianapolis Colts,

Tony Dungy speaks of the endless preparation that goes into winning a Super Bowl. He speaks of the time that the general manager of the Indianapolis Colts contacted him about serving as their head coach:

> "When Jim Irsay called he told me, 'I want you to be our coach and help us win the Super Bowl.' He told me, 'We are going to win it the right way. We are going to win it with great guys; win it with class and dignity. We are going to win it in a way that will make Indianapolis proud."

Five years later, Tony Dungy led the Colts to an NFL championship with their victory over the Chicago Bears in Super Bowl XLI.

For NFL players and coaches, it's all about the Super Bowl.   Hall of Fame former NFL coach and Super Bowl winner, Bill Parcells, famously said, "Even now, when Super Bowl time comes around, I get jealous.

Playing in the Super Bowl is an extravagant Someday, but every Someday is special and often can prove life changing. I chose the Super Bowl as a great example of a defining event that 32 football teams strive to participate in every year. The thrill of playing in such a celebratory game as that is an experience that every player who has ever walked out on the field Super Bowl Sunday will remember.

Although the vast majority of us will never play in a

Super Bowl, but there is a Someday that nearly all of us pursue at some point in our lifetime. That is the dream of meeting the man or woman of our dreams. Finding our one true love is life changing and unlike the Super Bowl, it's not just a single day, it can be for the rest of our lives.

Love is nothing to short change. As Ione Skye said in the movie, Dream for an Insomniac:

> "Unless it's mad, passionate, extraordinary love, it's a waste of your time. There are too many mediocre things in life. Love shouldn't be one of them."

Two years ago, my friend, Justin, called and literally blew up my phone with an endless stream of text messages and phone calls about a girl, not just any girl, a girl named Rachael who instantly changed his life forever. Justin had always been unlucky in love, and even in his mid-forties, he was still trying to find the woman who would become his wife. After one of his dates with Rachael early in the relationship, he wrote her the following email:

Dearest Rachael:

Historians define history by BC and AD. After yesterday, there is BKR and AKR (Before Kissing Rachael and After Kissing Rachael) now in my life, and it is from those points that I must reference time now.

I kissed you yesterday. I held you yesterday. I stared at your face yesterday, and suddenly I realized that there is now a BKR and AKR. I realized that after experiencing your kiss, which still lingers on my lips, I want to tell people about you--to brag about you. I want to walk into a bar with your picture, showing strangers your photo, telling them that this gorgeous woman was just in my arms. I want to climb to the highest skyscraper and shout out to the city that I think Rachael likes me.

It is Tuesday morning, and I wish I was holding you, staring at your face, and experiencing your kiss. I wish I had a confidant that I could tell how I love when your hair falls over your left eye and how when I push back your hair, I can see your entire face and soak it in. I could tell them about your eyes, about your skin, and about your lips. I'd probably get frustrated because my mind hasn't been able to memorize every millimeter of your face yet, so I couldn't tell them about everything. But that's a good thing, because it means I have hours and hours more to stare at you and memorize your features.

That was a day that still redefines his life, and a day that changed him forever. It took him decades to meet her, and he swears it was worth every lonely moment he spent now that he finally found her. They are soon going to marry, and they are writing their own vows in which he pledges to never take her, or her love, for granted. His planned vocation is to make every day with her a honeymoon. You may scoff at that statement, but then you have never seen a man as joyous as Justin. He is living his Someday with Rachael each and every day. (Rachael of coursed still treasures this email to this day and the two of them still celebrate AKR day every year)

When it comes to love, everyday can be Someday!

During the pursuit of your Someday, there will be days you realize you aren't going down the right path, and that you need to navigate another path towards your Someday. There will be days you realize you may need a whole new game plan. There will be days where it seems like you may never see the fruition of your dream. And on those days, focus on the idea that your Someday may be more than just a single event. It could mean the total transformation of your life. Like the day Jerry met Rachael, it could be the first day of a celebration that will last every day of your life.

Accomplishing one's dreams requires determination. Determination can be summed up as the unyielding perseverance to succeed. And through relentless determination, your Someday may be the determining factor that puts you on the world's largest stage on Super Bowl Sunday, or changes your life forever into a life comprised of infinite daily doses of joy as you spend time with the one you love.

Remember, Someday is a great day!

Attitude is Everything

"We can complain because rose bushes have thorns, or rejoice because thorn bushes have roses."

- Abraham Lincoln

Writing this book has proved a wonderful distraction from dealing with my beloved Atlanta Falcons this football season. After finishing the 2012 football season with a 13 – 3 record, they clinched home field advantage throughout the playoffs. As a season ticket holder, I attended both playoff games that January, including the NFC Championship game where I watched the Falcons come up just a couple of plays short of going to the Super Bowl. It was a tough loss that night but like many fans who left the stadium afterwards, I was confident that we would be Super Bowl bound next season and finally win the big one.

What a difference a year makes. As of this week, we have only won two out of eleven games this season and hold the title of last place in our division with no chance of making the playoffs. In fact, we are tied for last place in the entire NFL which will at least garner us an early draft pick five months from now.

So what happened? Sports talk radio here in Georgia

is trying to answer this question on a daily basis. Whatever the reason may be, the truth is that the Falcons probably weren't as good as their record boasted last year, nor are they as bad as their losses indicate this year. Attitude has most certainly played a role in this tale of two seasons.

A series of early victories certainly gave the team confidence last season, which created momentum that allotted them that extra boost to pull out a number of narrow victories last year in the final moments. In contrast, a couple of crippling early defeats this season combined with season-ending injuries to a couple of key players probably broke the confidence of the team and soured any hopes and aspirations of playing in the Super Bowl.

Attitude is everything.

I was having a conversation with some friends the other night about the stock market. They were struggling for reasons as to why the stock market was continuing to surge upwards despite a seemingly weak economy. They started talking about price/earnings ratios and other technical jargon when I kindly interrupted them and stated that it has nothing to do with any of that. The stock market is going up because there are more buyers than sellers and the reason people buy a particular stock is they have a positive attitude about it. They buy it because they see the stock price going higher. As soon as they have a negative attitude about the market, it will go down, and drop quickly. It's really just as simple as that.

This simplicity was vividly illustrated in the stock crash of 1929. The stock market tumbled 11% on October 24th of that year, a day otherwise known as Black Thursday. That day was the first of a four-day period in which the market plunged an astounding 25%. The market subsequently lost a total of 90% of its value between its record high close of 381.2 on September 3, 1929, and its subsequent bottom of 41.22 on July 8, 1932.

So what happened? The roaring 20's had produced a vibrant thriving economy of which the stock market benefited greatly, enjoying a nearly 400% return between 1926 and 1929. Stocks such as that of U.S. Steel were considered to be completely stable and reliable. U.S. Steel was known as the widower's stock because widows knew that if they put the money left to them by their departed husbands into their stock, that U.S. Steel would take care of their money. Investors believed in stocks such as U.S. Steel because of their strong brand recognition, wonderful products and competent management.

So why did people start dumping these highly coveted stocks in wild disarray all of a sudden? The brand hadn't changed, the product line was just as sound and the same management remained. Only one thing had changed . . .

The attitude of investors.

The housing crash that began in 2006 is another example. Just prior to the crash, home buyers were bidding up prices in a total frenzy to get into a home, no matter what the price. After all, everyone knew that home prices never go down, right? Only a few years later, home prices plunged across the country, as much as 40% in some markets as homes remained on the market for months on end with no hope of a buyer. Suddenly, no one wanted to buy a home. Why was this? The street address of these homes hadn't changed so they remained in the same school district. They still contained the same number of bedrooms and boasted the same stainless steel appliances and granite countertops. Nothing had changed . . .

Except the attitude of home buyers.

People's attitudes matter, and unfortunately they can fluctuate like the wind. Attitude plays a key role in the success or failure of a sports team. Attitude is a key driver of the economy, both at a macro and micro level. Attitude plays an active part in nearly every facet of life.

And your attitude plays a very important role in the pursuit of your Someday! It is the most important tool you have in your arsenal. A positive attitude can augment your efforts, giving you the momentum necessary to get you over the finish line and see your dreams through to the end. A negative attitude can magnify your setbacks and it doesn't take long for everything to come crashing down fairly quickly. Unfortunately, a negative attitude can do a lot of damage in a very short amount of time. A positive attitude is like a staircase that slowly directs you upwards towards your goal step-by-step. A negative attitude is a single step that can send you falling off the cliff and destroy months if not years of progress in one swoop.

So, if Someday is great day, and attitude is everything, then managing your attitude is imperative to staying on task and seeing the goal through. Always have a positive attitude about Someday, and one day soon, you will celebrate the greatness of that day.

Now Go Do It

"Our history is not our destiny."

- Alan Cohen, author

We create our own destiny. We alone decide the direction our life. Yesterday is the past and your Someday is just around the corner. Let's review what we've discussed about your Someday and how to see it become reality.

- Like a lustrous pearl clenched in your hand, your Someday is valuable, it gives you direction in life and gives you a sense of purpose in your daily life. Feel yourself lucky that you have a dream, that you have a Someday to look forward to because so many people around you don't.

- A wish is not a Someday. A wish requires a magical genie to appear. A Someday is a dream that only requires your determination and the implementation of a plan to make that Someday a reality.

- If you find yourself relentlessly talking about your Someday but never doing anything about it, imagine how weary all of your friends and family are constantly hearing about it. The time for merely talking about it is over. It's time to devise a plan and implement it.

- Every plan needs a time table. Nothing gets done without setting a date, a target on your calendar that will keep you disciplined and focused. Set a date right now and stick to it.

- Rethink your vocabulary. Forget about phrases such as "I Should" and replace them with phrases such as "I Will."

- Remember you can't negotiate with Father Time. You only get so many heartbeats in this world and you and only you decide what you spend them on.

- Most people associate dreams with accomplishments, but a dream may simply be to simply your life or do absolutely nothing at all Someday.

- If you are a young person, then don't feel obligated to go about your life in the same cookie cutter formula that your peers, relatives or society levies on you. Feel free to navigate your own path as there are many ways to get to Someday.

- If you're in your 50's, learn from the big mistake you made when you were younger, that you only get so many years of youthfulness. Also take note that, once the kids are gone and you are rid of many other obligations, that you will have many of the same advantages you enjoyed in your 20's that will allow you to focus more directly on your Someday.

- Make yourself aware of the endless opportunities that lie around you. They are everywhere, but often times can only be recognized by putting your nose to the ground and getting directly involved with your surroundings.

- If your Someday involves another person, be aware that this means that you can't do it all and try as you may, no matter how much energy and effort you exert, it will never make up for their lack of commitment. Unless the other person is actively partaking in the journey with you, it may be time to move one at some point.

- It pays to be optimistic, for optimism is what fuels dreams and keep us going, even on the darkest of days. But blind optimism is worse than no optimism. You will have to make a number of decisions throughout the process of attaining your Someday and you must base those decisions on the realistic factual information around you.

- Stop engaging in the impossible task of trying to make everyone around you happy. Even the greatest spiritual and political leaders of the world can't do that. You only have so much energy and time each and every day so don't spend it all on everyone else.

- Remember the old adage, you don't own your stuff, it owns you. All of that stuff you have in your house that you "think" you need requires maintenance, time and attention and may be hampering you from achieving your Someday. Movement is life.

- Know how to say No. Sure you have to perform the natural obligations of family, work and community, but you have to focus on yourself as well. Helping others makes one feel good and stewardship is a noble quality that adds to one's sense of happiness, but don't treat it like a forever running spigot. Know when to turn it off from time to time so you can get stuff done yourself.

- Know that there are going to be setbacks. Rome wasn't built in a day and there are bound to be some unforeseen obstacles along the way and even pitfalls in our journey to Someday. Don't be discouraged however. Dust yourself and bear through it, and if the situation at hand seems too daunting, focus on how wonderful your Someday is going to be. Remember, Someday is a great day.

And finally, in the words of the popular Nike Slogan,

Just do it!

Enjoy Someday

ABOUT THE AUTHOR

Brad Rudisail is a writer, musician and IT Consultant. Brad was a syndicated writer for eleven years writing a bi-monthly column for newspapers throughout the state of Georgia. He is a hired blogger and writes educational curriculum for online universities. He is an accomplished pianist and composer and has won regional and national awards for his musical work and has released six instrumental CD's throughout his career. He is also an IT consultant and serves a variety of clients across the globe as a network engineer and trainer.

You can read more about Brad and view more of his readings about the subject of this book at
www.SomedayIAmGoingTo.com.

If you enjoyed this book, please feel free to write a review on Amazon as reviews help a great deal in marketing the book. Thanks in advance.

www.ingramcontent.com/pod-product-compliance
Lightning Source LLC
Chambersburg PA
CBHW061736020426
42331CB00006B/1256